Using the
Schoolwide
Enrichment
Model  in Mathematics

Using the
Schoolwide
Enrichment
Model in Mathematics

A How-to Guide for Developing Student Mathematicians

M. Katherine Gavin, Ph.D., &
Joseph S. Renzulli, Ed.D.

PRUFROCK PRESS INC.
WACO, TEXAS

Library of Congress catalog information
currently on file with the publisher.

Copyright ©2018, Prufrock Press Inc.

Edited by Katy McDowall

Cover and layout design by Allegra Denbo

ISBN-13: 978-1-61821-748-6

Printed in the United States of America.

At the time of this book's publication, all facts and figures cited are the most current available. All telephone numbers, addresses, and website URLs are accurate and active. All publications, organizations, websites, and other resources exist as described in the book, and all have been verified. The authors and Prufrock Press Inc. make no warranty or guarantee concerning the information and materials given out by organizations or content found at websites, and we are not responsible for any changes that occur after this book's publication. If you find an error, please contact Prufrock Press Inc.

Prufrock Press Inc.
P.O. Box 8813
Waco, TX 76714-8813
Phone: (800) 998-2208
Fax: (800) 240-0333
http://www.prufrock.com

Table of Contents

A Note to Our Readers

We wrote this book just for you. We hope you will use it as the title indicates, as a how-to guide to create what we affectionately call the Three Es of learning—enjoyment, engagement, and enthusiasm—with your students in math class.

This book is not a math curriculum such as that which you would find in a typical grade-level textbook. Rather, it is a supplementary set of recommended teaching strategies and resources that will allow you to infuse various enrichment experiences and high-level content into any and all math curricula that may be prescribed by existing textbooks or lists of standards used in your school district. This book was designed to provide instructional strategies and curriculum resources that will enhance whatever math curriculum you have adopted.

Instruction provided in the math curriculum is the "raw material" of learning, and we can enhance prescribed curriculum through hands-on activities, selected enrichment resources, and an investigative mindset. Strengthening your students' enjoyment, engagement, and enthusiasm for learning will make your classroom a more exciting place and help your students see the role and relevance of math instruction. We hope learning about the Enrichment Triad Model in math, along with views from the classroom that show how teachers put ideas into action, will inspire you.

We wish you and your students upcoming math classes filled with enjoyment, engagement, and enthusiasm.

—Kathy and Joe

CHAPTER 1

Overview of the Schoolwide Enrichment Model

The Schoolwide Enrichment Model: A Focus on Student Strengths and Interests

Most of our work on the Schoolwide Enrichment Model (SEM) has been devoted to research and development on identification practices and teaching strategies for promoting gifted behaviors. Over the years, we realized that many students, in addition to those formally identified as gifted, could benefit from school experiences that are more enriching, engaging, and challenging. We also realized that in order to make changes in entire schools we needed to pay some attention to an organizational plan or model for the delivery of these strategies and the professional development that is guided by our theories and research. The SEM is not intended to replace existing gifted education programs. Rather, it is designed to infuse various types of enrichment into all aspects of the curriculum and to make certain types of enrichment activities available to the larger school population. We believe that a total talent development model must look at the mission, culture, and commitment of entire schools in addition to what goes on in special programs. This approach to applying the pedagogy of gifted education to total talent development is a departure from most traditional approaches that focus only on identified gifted students. Although there has been some criticism from persons representing more conservative positions in the field, national interests in both promoting 21st-century skills for all students and the need to

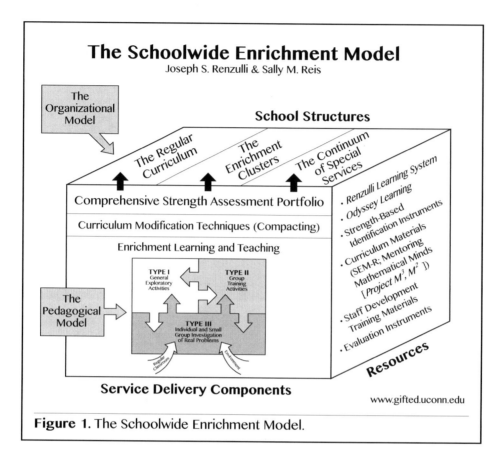

Figure 1. The Schoolwide Enrichment Model.

recognize talent potentials in underrepresented groups have resulted in a growing number of adoptions of the programming model presented in this book. The chapters that follow cover major components of the model as applied to the field of mathematics. An overview of the model is presented in Figure 1, and you will note here that the three major service delivery components of the SEM are brought to bear on three school organizational structures. These service delivery components, as they relate to mathematics, will be discussed in the chapters that follow.

In this chapter we provide an overview of the Schoolwide Enrichment Model and recommend that interested readers examine the third edition of *The Schoolwide Enrichment Model: A How-to Guide for Talent Development* (Renzulli & Reis, 2014) for detailed information about implementing the model. This book contains several instruments and planning guides that can be reproduced with permission for individual use.

What's a Model?

Before providing this overview of the SEM, it might be worthwhile to reflect for a moment about the meaning and purpose of this or any other plan that is designed to bring about selected changes in a school and the ways in which educators serve young people. The first consideration in answering the above question is the distinction between two categories of educational models. We will refer to the first category as administrative models and the second as theoretical models.

Administrative models consist of patterns of school organization and procedures for dealing with such issues as how educators group students, develop schedules, and allocate time, money, and human resources. Administrative models focus mainly on how educators group students and "move them around" and how they arrange for the delivery of services. Issues dealt with in administrative models might include homogeneous versus heterogeneous grouping, length of the school day or year, inclusion of special education students in regular classrooms, and whether or not educators should use a resource room or within-the-classroom program for the gifted.

Theoretical or pedagogical models, on the other hand, focus on the ways that educators provide the actual services to students, regardless of the manner in which they organize their schools or school schedules. Theoretical models consist of principles that guide the learning process and give direction to the content of the curriculum, the assessment and instructional strategies that teachers use, and ways in which educators evaluate the extent and quality of what their students have learned. Theoretical models focus on the actual outcomes of learning experiences that might take place within any given administrative pattern of organization. Theoretical models are influential in determining the quality of school experiences, whereas administrative models are more concerned with the efficiency and "smoothness" of the school's operation.

Although the SEM has certain implications for organizational patterns, we consider it a theoretically based model because it is guided by the Enrichment Triad Model (Renzulli, 1977a) that is based on: (1) a series of assumptions about individual differences in learners and the use of strength-based assessment, (2) research-based principles of learning, and (3) recommended practices that logically follow from these assumptions and principles. A crucial consideration in selecting this or any other model is whether or not there is a consensus among teachers, parents, and administrators about the assumptions, principles, and recommended practices. We have found that when such a consensus exists, most schools easily accomplish the relatively small organizational or administrative changes necessary for implementing the model. Our experience has also shown that a theoretical model that infuses instructional practices into existing administrative patterns of organization has a higher probability of success and sustainability than an approach that tries to completely reorganize the school.

A Brief History of the Schoolwide Enrichment Model

How do we view and develop gifted behaviors in young people? How can we develop the potential of all children? What services should be provided to students who are identified for gifted and talented programs that would also provide some enrichment services to all students who can benefit from more engaging and challenging school experiences? Can enrichment programs for all students help to increase academic achievement scores? Can creative productivity be enhanced when students participate in enrichment or gifted education programs? How can we help children learn to think creatively and value opportunities for creative, self-selected work?

The Schoolwide Enrichment Model was developed to address these questions through a focus on developing gifted behaviors and creative productivity in young people. Although innovation is typically viewed as a process that always begins with a creative idea and ends with new or improved products, there are other factors that contribute to designing purposive tasks that can be organized into systematic plans for transforming ideas into tangible outcomes. In this chapter we discuss three interrelated components of creative productivity—above-average ability in a particular domain, creativity, and task commitment. The interaction between and among these components of the innovative process is necessary to provide the strategies for developing products or performances that can become audience- or consumer-valued products. Next, we discuss three types of educational services for promoting innovation in young people. These services consist of exposing students to areas of potential interest and task commitment, providing them with the methodological skills to pursue their interests in a professionally authentic manner, and providing the opportunities, resources, and encouragement to see their ideas through to fruition.

The two following examples of the model at work in mathematics will give you a practical understanding of the model in action.

As a 10th grader, Amber experimented with the mathematical equations used to calculate changes in space and time near black holes, and then shared this information via the Internet with physicists in other parts of the world. This talent for logical and insightful thinking was recognized and validated for Amber when scientists provided constructive feedback for her ideas, helping her to obtain new knowledge and skills as well as providing her with an outlet for synthesizing information about this topic. Several websites provide opportunities to "ask the experts." With the help of scientists on the *Scientific American* website (https://www.scientificamerican.com/section/ask-the-experts), Amber became interested in specific calculations related to the black hole phenomenon. She entered her mathematical calculations about this topic in a local science fair competition and was awarded an honorable mention at the state level for her precision in and explanation of her calculations. As a result of her project, she also developed a website to teach other students about astronomy and space travel.

At age 17, Chris's interest in engineering led to his acceptance in a competitive summer internship at a university well known for its faculty who conduct scientific research. Paired with a scientist in chemical engineering, Chris was assigned a project to investigate cancer cell growth. During the 7-week internship, he researched the topic, wrote a program in a computer language he had barely used before, solved the mathematical problem given to him about the growth of a particular cancer cell, and then crafted and presented a paper entitled "Computer Simulations and Cancer Research: A New Solution to a Complex Problem?"

The ability to develop innovative ideas can begin at an early age and evolve over time. These students have multiple characteristics in common, namely, the capacity to work intensely on a specific topic, to apply their natural inclinations and ability toward a specific activity, and to create something that they want to share with others, particularly with an audience who appreciates the topic. Although Amber is still establishing her knowledge base in the field of black holes, she is able to produce sound ideas and questions that have received pointed responses from international experts who are nurturing her understanding of astronomy and physics. Her science fair submission and her website represent outlets for sharing her work with others. Chris also created new products, which he disseminated to the public. Children and young adults have the ability to be more than consumers of information. They can be creative producers of high-quality products (Delcourt, 2008; Renzulli, 1986; Renzulli & Reis, 1985). To help youths achieve this goal, we need to recognize the characteristics that lead to innovative behaviors and provide the type of environment that is a catalyst for these endeavors.

The Three-Ring Conception of Giftedness

The underlying theory about how we view and define gifted behaviors is called the Three-Ring Conception of Giftedness (Renzulli, 1978). Research on creative productive people has consistently shown that although no single criterion can be used to determine giftedness, individuals who have achieved recognition because of their unique accomplishments and creative contributions possess a relatively well-defined set of three interlocking clusters of traits. These clusters consist of above-average, although not necessarily superior, ability; task commitment; and creativity (see Figure 2). It is important to point out that no single cluster "makes giftedness." Rather, it is the interaction among the three clusters that researchers have shown to be the necessary ingredient for creative productive accomplishment (Renzulli, 1978). This interaction is represented by the shaded portion in the center of Figure 2. It is also important to indicate that each cluster plays an important role in contributing to the display of gifted behaviors. This point is emphasized because one of the major errors that educators continue to make in identification procedures is to overemphasize superior abilities at the expense of the other two clusters of traits. The background of this diagram, referred to as a "houndstooth" pattern, represents the interaction between internal (personality) and external (environmental) characteristics that influence each individual.

Above-Average Ability

Above-average ability can be defined in two ways. One view includes the broad concept of overall capacity to think and perform, although the other perspective targets particular ways in which an individual understands, interprets, and reacts to information in a specialized domain (Csikszentmihalyi, 1990; Renzulli, 2005; Treffinger, 1998).

General ability consists of the capacity to process information, to integrate experiences that result in appropriate and adaptive responses in new situations, and the capacity to engage in abstract thinking. Examples of general ability are verbal and numerical reasoning, spatial relations, memory, and word fluency.

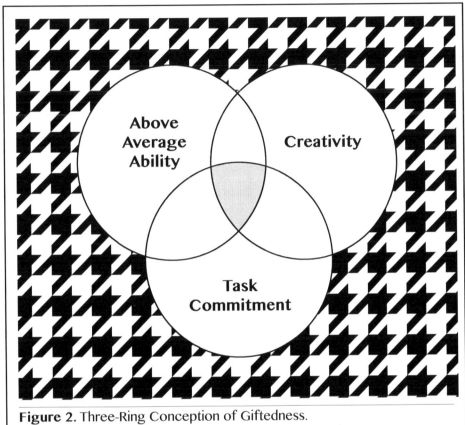

Figure 2. Three-Ring Conception of Giftedness.

These abilities are usually measured by tests of general aptitude or intelligence, and are broadly applicable to a variety of traditional learning situations. The following are examples of general abilities (Renzulli & Reis, 2014):

› High levels of abstract thinking, verbal and numerical reasoning, spatial relations, memory, and word fluency.

› Adaption to and the shaping of novel situations encountered in the external environment.

› The automatization of information processing. Rapid, accurate, and selective retrieval of information. (p. 23)

Specific abilities consist of the capacity to acquire knowledge, skill, or the capacity to perform in one or more activities of a specialized kind and within a restricted range, as indicated in the following examples (Renzulli & Reis, 2014):

› The application of various combinations of the general abilities listed above to one or more specialized areas of knowledge or areas of human performance (e.g., the arts, leadership, administration).

> › The capacity for acquiring and making appropriate use of advanced amounts of formal knowledge, tacit knowledge, technique, logistics, and strategy in the pursuit of particular problems or the manifestation of specialized areas of performance.
> › The capacity to sort out relevant and irrelevant information associated with a particular problem or area of study or performance. (p. 23)

These abilities are defined according to the ways in which human beings express themselves in real-life (i.e., nontest) situations. Examples of specific abilities are chemistry, ballet, mathematics, musical composition, sculpture, and photography. Specific abilities can be further subdivided into even more specific areas (e.g., portrait photography, astrophotography, photo journalism, etc.). Specific abilities in certain areas such as mathematics and chemistry have a strong relationship with general ability, and some indication of potential in these areas can therefore be determined from tests of general aptitude and intelligence. Achievement tests of specific aptitudes and actual examples of students' work—what is commonly referred to as performance-based assessment — can also help identify talent. Looking for behavioral characteristics that mimic the processes mathematicians and scientists use is also valuable in identifying potential in these areas. These characteristics can help identify students who have creative-productive potential, the ones who have the ability to contribute new theories and discoveries in mathematics and science. Many specific abilities, however, do not even have tests that are specifically designed to help measure potential or achievement associated with them.

Within this model, the term *above-average ability* is used to describe both general and specific abilities. *Above-average* should also be interpreted to mean the upper range of potential within any given area. Although it is difficult to assign numerical values to many specific areas of ability, "well-above-average ability" refers to persons who are capable of performance or the potential for performance that is representative of the top 15%–20% of any given area of human endeavor. This is the population typically represented in 4-year college enrollment.

Task Commitment

A second cluster of traits that has consistently been found in creative productive persons is a refined or focused form of motivation known as task commitment. Examples include the following (Renzulli & Reis, 2014):

› The capacity for high levels of interest, enthusiasm, fascination, and involvement in a particular problem, area of study, or form of human expression.

› The capacity for perseverance, endurance, determination, hard work, and dedicated practice.

› Self-confidence, a strong ego, and a belief in one's ability to carry out important work, freedom from inferiority feelings, and drive to achieve.

› The ability to identify significant problems within specialized areas. The ability to tune in to major channels of communication and new developments within given fields.

› Setting high standards for one's work, maintaining openness to self- and external criticism, developing an aesthetic sense of taste, quality, and excellence about one's own work and the work of others. (p. 23)

Whereas motivation is usually defined in terms of a general energizing process that triggers responses in organisms, task commitment represents energy brought to bear on a particular problem (task) or specific performance area. The terms most frequently used to describe task commitment are perseverance or grit, endurance, hard work, dedicated practice, and self-confidence in one's ability to carry out important work.

Creativity

The third cluster of traits that characterize persons who display gifted behaviors consists of factors usually lumped together under the general heading of "creativity." The following are examples of creative abilities (Renzulli & Reis, 2014):

› Fluency, flexibility, and originality of thought.

› Openness to experience; receptiveness to that which is new and different (even irrational) in the thoughts, actions, and products of oneself and others.

› Curious, speculative, adventurous, and "mentally playful." Willing to take risks in thought and action, even to the point of being uninhibited.

› Sensitive to detail, aesthetic characteristics of ideas and things. Willing to act on and react to external stimulation and one's own ideas and feelings. (p. 23)

As one reviews the literature in this area, it becomes readily apparent that the words *gifted, genius, innovators,* and *eminent creators* or *highly creative persons* are used interchangeably. In many of the research studies designed to understand the characteristics of innovative individuals, those ultimately selected for intensive study were in fact recognized because of their creative accomplishments (Bloom & Sosniak, 1981; MacKinnon, 1964; McCurdy, 1960; Nicholls, 1972).

Above-average ability, task commitment, and creativity are the types of characteristics we are looking for in people who are known to be or will be innovators. Students who manifest or are capable of developing an interaction among these three clusters require a wide variety of educational opportunities, resources, and encouragement above and beyond those ordinarily provided through regular instructional programs.

Identification of Students With the Potential for Innovation

The Three-Ring Conception of Giftedness was reported to be one of the most prevalent models for identifying potentially gifted or innovative students in the United States (Callahan, Hunsaker, Adams, Moore, & Bland, 1995). School personnel who use this model typically employ one or more instruments that represent each of the three rings. Ideally, multiple instruments and sources of data are used to target students who are capable of creative productive behavior. Specific processes for identifying these students can be found in supplementary references (Renzulli, 1994). The following sections of this chapter focus on methods used to develop and enhance characteristics of innovative behavior in children and young adults.

The Dual Goal of Developing Academic Giftedness and Creative Productivity

Present efforts to develop giftedness are based on a long history of previous theoretical or research studies dealing with human abilities (Gardner, 1983, 2008, 2011; Sternberg, 1984, 1988, 1990; Sternberg & Davidson, 1986; Thorndike, 1921) and a few general conclusions from the most current research on giftedness (Sternberg & Davidson, 2005), which provide critical background for this discussion of the SEM. The first essential understanding is that giftedness is not a unitary concept, but rather, that students possess many manifestations of gifts and talents, and therefore, single definitions cannot adequately explain this multifaceted phenomenon. The confusion about present theories of giftedness has led many researchers to develop new models for explaining this complicated concept, but most agree that giftedness is developed over time and that culture, abilities, environment, gender, opportunities, and chance contribute to the development of gifts and talents (Sternberg & Davidson, 2005).

The SEM focuses on the development of both academic and creative productive giftedness. Creative productive giftedness describes those aspects of human activity and involvement where a premium is placed on the development of original material and products that are purposefully designed to have an impact on one or more target audiences. Learning situations designed to promote creative productive giftedness emphasize the use and application of information (content) and thinking skills in an integrated, inductive, and real-problem-oriented manner. In the SEM, traditional academic strengths are developed using curriculum compacting, grade skipping, differentiated instruction, enrichment clusters, cluster grouping (Gentry, 2014), afterschool programs, and various forms of academic enrichment. Our focus on creative productivity complements our efforts to increase academic challenge when we attempt to transform the role of the student from that of a learner of lessons to one of a firsthand inquirer who can experience the joys and frustrations of creative productivity (Renzulli, 1977a). This approach is quite different from the development of giftedness that tends to emphasize deductive learning, advanced content and problem solving, and the acquisition, storage, and retrieval of information. In other words, creative productive giftedness enables children to work on issues and areas of study that have personal relevance to the students and can be escalated to appropriately challenging levels of investigative activity.

Why is creative productive giftedness important enough to question the traditional approach that has been used to select students for gifted programs on the basis of test scores? Why do some people want to rock the boat by challenging a conception of giftedness that can be numerically defined by simply giving a test? The answers to these questions are simple and yet compelling. A review of research literature (Neisser, 1979; Reis & Renzulli, 1982; Renzulli, 1978, 1986, 2005) tells us that there is much more to identifying human potential than the abilities revealed on traditional tests of intelligence, aptitude, and achievement. Furthermore, history tells us it has been the creative and productive people of the world, the producers rather than consumers of knowledge, who have been recognized in history as "truly gifted" individuals. Accordingly, the SEM integrates both opportunities for academic giftedness, as well as creative productive giftedness.

Understanding the Service Delivery Components of the SEM

The three major service delivery components on the face of the cube in Figure 1 are designed to be brought to bear on the three school structures at the top of the diagram.

Comprehensive Strength Assessment

The first component, comprehensive strength assessment, is achieved by compiling a Total Talent Portfolio for each student that includes information from achievement tests, teacher ratings of potential for creativity and task commitment (Renzulli, Hartman, & Callahan, 1971; Renzulli, 1977b), as well as self-ratings that students complete about their interests, learning styles (Renzulli & Sullivan, 2009), and preferred modes of expression (Kettle, Renzulli, & Rizza, 1998). A parent questionnaire that we have developed can be used for gathering information about things that students have accomplished in nonschool environments (Renzulli, Foreman, & Brandon, 2017).

Interest questionnaires cover the full range of academic areas as well as questions about topics in which students may have interests that are outside traditional academic areas. Learning style preferences include: projects, independent study, teaching games, simulations, peer teaching, computer-assisted instruction, lecture, drill and recitation, and discussion. Expression style preferences (e.g., verbal, written, oral, constructed, digital, mathematical, and artistic) are also analyzed, and a Total Talent Portfolio that focuses on student strengths rather than deficits should be completed for all students.

Curriculum Modification Techniques

This second service delivery component addresses the needs of students who achieve at higher levels than their peers in one or more academic areas. This type of differentiation is an attempt to address the variation of learners in the classroom through multiple approaches that modify instruction and curriculum to match the individual needs of students (Renzulli, 1977a; Tomlinson, 2000). Students within a classroom will vary in their abilities, interests, and prior knowledge. Differentiation serves to mitigate this variation by matching the instruction and assessment to the student's needs and interests. Tomlinson (1995) emphasized that when teachers differentiate curriculum, they stop acting as dispensers of knowledge and serve as organizers of learning opportunities. Differentiation of instruction and curriculum suggests that students can be provided with materials and work of varied levels of difficulty with scaffolding (social mediated instruction), diverse kinds of grouping, and different time schedules (Tomlinson, 2000). In other words, differentiation is the antithesis of one-size-fits-all curriculum.

Renzulli (1977a, 1988; Renzulli & Reis, 1997) defined differentiation as encompassing five dimensions: content, process, products, classroom organization and management, and the teacher's own commitment to change him- or herself into a learner as well as a teacher. The differentiation of content involves adding more depth (Renzulli, 2012) to the curriculum by focusing on structures of knowledge, basic principles, functional concepts, and methods of inquiry in particular disciplines. The differentiation of process incorporates the use of various instructional strategies and materials to enhance and motivate various students' learning styles. The differentiation of products enhances students' communication skills by encouraging them to express themselves in a variety of ways. To differentiate classroom management, teachers can change the physical environment and grouping patterns they use in class and vary the allocation of time and resources for both groups and individuals. Classroom differentiation strategies can also be greatly enhanced by using the Internet in a variety of creative ways. The Internet can expand the learning environment far beyond the walls of the classroom and offer particular promise for engaging and differentiating content for children. Finally, teachers can differentiate themselves by modeling the roles of athletic or drama coaches, stage or production managers, promotional agents, and academic advisers. All of these roles differ qualitatively from the role of teacher-as-instructor. Teachers can also "inject" themselves into the material through a process called artistic modification (Renzulli, 1988). This process guides teachers in the sharing of direct, indirect, and vicarious experiences related to personal interests, travel experiences, collections, hobbies, and teachers' "extra-curricular" involvements that can enhance content.

The Enrichment Triad Model

The third service delivery component of the SEM represents the pedagogy or learning theory described as the Enrichment Triad Model (Renzulli, 1977a). Often employed as an educational programming model for gifted and talented students, the Enrichment Triad Model is based upon activities and experiences that enhance the regular curriculum to promote creative productive behaviors, leading to innovative ideas and solutions to problems. The model can be presented in a sequence or employed as needed for individuals, small groups, or whole classes of students. The Triad promotes engagement for all students through the use of three types of enrichment experiences that are enjoyable, challenging, and interest-based. Separate studies on the Triad and the SEM have demonstrated its effectiveness in schools with widely differing socioeconomic levels and program organization patterns (Olenchak, 1988; Olenchak & Renzulli, 1989). The SEM was developed using the Enrichment Triad Model (Renzulli, 1977a; Renzulli & Reis, 1985, 1997) as a core along with other components, such as enrichment clusters and curriculum compacting. The effectiveness of the SEM has been studied in more than 40 years of research and field-tests, suggesting that the model is effective at serving high-potential students and providing enrichment in a variety of educational settings for all students, including schools serving culturally diverse and low socioeconomic status (SES) populations (Field, 2009; Gubbins, 1995; Reis, Eckert, McCoach, Jacobs, & Coyne, 2008; Reis & Renzulli, 2003; Renzulli & Delisle, 1982; Renzulli & Reis, 1994).

The original Enrichment Triad Model (see Figure 3), the curriculum core of the SEM, was developed in the mid-1970s and initially implemented as a gifted and talented programming model in many diverse school districts throughout the country. Note in Figure 3 that we recommend certain types of general enrichment (Types I and II and enrichment clusters) for all students, and opportunities for Type III Enrichment should be provided when students respond positively to general enrichment, the regular school curriculum, and topics that may originate from nonschool interests or the environment in general.

The model, initially field-tested in several districts, proved to be quite popular, and requests from all over the country for visitations to schools using the model, as well as for information about how to implement the model, increased. A book about the Enrichment Triad Model (Renzulli, 1977a) was published, and increasing numbers of districts began implementing this approach. It was, at this point, that a clear need was established for research regarding the effectiveness of the model, as well as for other vehicles that could provide technical assistance for interested educators to help develop programs in their schools. Different types of programs based on the Triad Model were designed and implemented by classroom teachers and gifted education specialists. Certain professional development opportunities and resources proved to be extremely helpful in enabling teachers to better implement the program, and we wondered how we could make these opportunities more readily available to larger numbers of teachers and students. And, of course, we became increasingly interested as to why the model was working and how we could further expand the research base

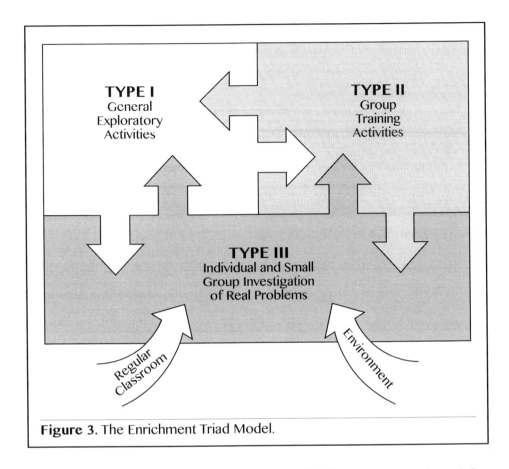

Figure 3. The Enrichment Triad Model.

of this approach. Thus began almost 40 years of field-testing, research, and dissemination. A brief overview of the Triad Model follows.

Type I Enrichment. This aspect of the model consists of general exploratory activities introducing a variety of topics not ordinarily available in the regular curriculum. A classroom can be organized to include a variety of experiences, including guest lecturers, demonstrations, interest development centers, book displays, introductory lessons, etc., which allow students exposure to new topics. Examples include the following:

› A local meteorologist presents information about climate change.
› A simulation is presented about animal migration.
› An interest development center is based on the works of the lithographer and painter M. C. Escher, where his works are displayed and activities are planned, which allow students to relate Escher's work to mathematics and to that of other artists.
› Books that introduce topics such as entomology, economics, physiology, poetry, etc., are added to the classroom library.

› The teacher introduces students to topics such as mystery story writing (language arts); "freakonomics" (Levitt & Dubner, 2005), which involves mathematics, economics, and political science; genealogy (social studies); etc.

Type I activities are appropriate for all students. Everyone should be given the opportunity to learn and think about new topics. Many children and adolescents lament their lack of interest in anything, mostly because they do not know about a great variety of topics. A series of instruments entitled *Interest-A-Lyzers* (Hébert, Sorensen, & Renzulli, 1997; Renzulli, 1997) are student inventories that offer many opportunities for young people to express what they would like to do by asking questions, such as "You are a famous author about to write your next book. What will it be about?" "Imagine that you can travel to any time in history. Where would you go?" "Have you ever made up a new game? Tell about it here." Responses to these and many other questions can help a student identify areas that are already strengths and locate new topics of interest.

An educator could choose an idea from the *Interest-A-Lyzer* and initiate or locate related presentations at a local library or target books that explain how to get involved with the selected topic. By introducing a student to a variety of ideas, he or she will be more likely to be able to choose an area of interest. Once a student focuses on a particular area, such as poetry, chemistry, bird watching, or cars, the next step is to find out the skills needed to pursue this topic. Beginning questions can include: "How do writers get their ideas for a poem?" "What equipment do I need to conduct a chemistry experiment?" "How can I identify the birds in my neighborhood?" "What steps should I take to design a blueprint for a car?"

Students, teachers, and parents can also use a computer-based program called Renzulli Learning (http://www.renzullilearning.com) in order to match student interests, learning styles, and expression styles with a variety of skill development activities and viable project ideas. All three types of enrichment activities can be accessed through this interactive program. After completing the student profiler, hundreds of websites will become available that target a student's interests and skills. The online educational program also promotes academic achievement as indicated by significant growth in reading comprehension, oral reading fluency, and achievement in social studies (Field, 2009). In addition, we have outlined a multitude of Type I experiences specifically for mathematics in Chapter 3.

Type II Enrichment. Type II activities introduce and strengthen training in thinking and feeling processes; learning how-to-learn skills; research and reference skills; written, oral, and visual communication skills; and metacognitive skills in technology. Figure 4 presents a breakdown of the areas into which we have classified various Type II skills.

Students and teachers will find many activities for developing skills of professionals in a wide variety of fields using Renzulli Learning. In addition, there are excellent resources for developing skills of young researchers (*Chi Square, Pie Charts, and Me* by Baum, Gable, & List, 1998; *Think Data* by Renzulli, Heilbronner, & Siegle, 2010; *Looking for Data in All the Right Places* by Starko & Schack, 1992); entrepreneurs (*The New Totally Awesome Business Book for Kids* by Bochner & Bochner, 2007); scientists (*Hands-on Ecology* by Kessler, 2006); writers (*How Writers Work* by Fletcher, 2000); and other professionals. Specific resources for developing the processes and skills of mathematicians will be found in subsequent chapters. The focus of these materials is to assist in the development of a variety of behaviors similar to those of a practicing professional in a given field of study, allowing students to rehearse and refine the skills necessary to produce high-quality, innovative projects. Chapters 4 and 5 are specifically focused on Type II experiences—learning and using the processes and skills that mathematicians employ in their work.

Type III Enrichment. This type of enrichment consists of individual and small-group investigations of real problems. We define "real problems" as creative or investigative projects that include the following four essential characteristics:

> › personalization of interest,
> › use of authentic methodology,
> › no existing solution or "right" answer, and
> › designed to have an impact on an audience other than, or in addition to, the teacher.

Type III projects differ from problem-based learning in that they meet all of the above listed criteria. The two mathematics projects that Amber and Chris created, which we described on page 7, are examples of such products. In Chapter 6, we explore a wide variety of Type III experiences in mathematics. Other examples might include:

> › reviving a wetlands area to attract more wildlife and presenting the project to a local environmental planning board for replication in multiple regions,
> › planting shrubbery to feed migrating animals and logging the progress of the migration in a national scientific database,

Taxonomy of Type II Enrichment Process Skills

I. COGNITIVE TRAINING

A. Creativity. Developing and Practicing the Use of:

Fluency	Brainstorming	Imagery
Flexibility	Forced Relationships	Association
Originality	Attribute Listing	Comparison
Elaboration	Fantasy	Risk Taking

Modification Techniques:

Adaptation	Substitution	Combination
Magnification	Multiple Uses	Reversal
Minification	Rearrangement	

B. Creative Problem Solving and Decision Making. Developing and Practicing the Use of:

Creative Problem Solving:

Mess Finding	Problem Finding	Solution Finding
Fact Finding	Idea Finding	Acceptance Finding

Decision Making:

Stating Desired Goals and Conditions Related to a Decision That Needs to Be Made
Stating the Obstacles to Realizing the Goals and Conditions
Identifying the Alternatives Available for Overcoming Each Obstacle
Examining Alternatives in Terms of Resources, Costs, Constraints, and Time
Ranking Alternatives in Terms of Probable Consequences
Choosing the Best Alternative
Evaluating the Actions Resulting From the Decision

C. Critical and Logical Thinking. Developing and Practicing the Use of:

Conditional Reasoning	Extrapolation	Dilemmas
Ambiguity	Patterning	Paradoxes
Fallacies	Sequencing	Analysis of:
Emotive Words	Flow Charting	- Content
Definition of Terms	Computer Programming	- Elements
Categorical Propositions	Analogies	- Trends and Patterns
Classification	Inferences	- Relationships
Validity Testing	Inductive Reasoning	- Organizing Principles
Reliability Testing	Deductive Reasoning	- Propaganda and Bias
Translation	Syllogisms	
Interpretation	Probability	

Figure 4. Taxonomy of Type II processes.
Note. The Taxonomies displayed this figure are not intended to be a complete listing of every thinking and feeling process, nor are the processes listed here mutually exclusive. Rather, there are many instances in which the processes interact with one another and even duplicate items from various categories. Because of this interaction and the need to use several processes simultaneously in their application to real problems, it is important to teach them in various combinations rather than in an item-by-item fashion. Whenever possible, we have attempted to list the process skills in a logical hierarchy, but it is important to point out that the appropriate use of thinking skills often proceeds in a cyclical rather than linear fashion. For this reason, it is not necessary to teach each set of skills in a rigidly sequential fashion; however, there may be instances when a sequence will facilitate comprehension and application.

II. AFFECTIVE TRAINING

Understanding Yourself
Understanding Others
Working With Groups
Peer Relationships
Parent Relationships
Values Clarification
Moral Reasoning
Sex Role Stereotypes
Assertiveness Training
Self-Reliance

Dealing With Conflict
Coping Behaviors
Analyzing Your Strengths
Planning Your Future
Interpersonal Communication
Developing Self-Confidence
Developing a Sense of Humor
Showing an Understanding of Others
Dealing With Fear, Anxiety and Guilt
Dealing With the Unknown

III. LEARNING HOW-TO-LEARN SKILLS

A. Listening, Observing, and Perceiving. Developing and Practicing the Use of:

Following Directions
Noting Specific Details
Understanding Main Points, Themes, and
  Sequences
Separating Relevant From Irrelevant
  Information
Paying Attention to Whole-Part Relationships
Scanning for the "Big Picture"

Focusing in on Particulars
Asking for Clarification
Asking Appropriate Questions
Making Inferences
Noting Subtleties
Predicting Outcomes
Evaluating a Speaker's Point of View

B. Notetaking and Outlining. Developing and Practicing the Use of:

Notetaking:
  Selecting Key Terms, Concepts, and Ideas
  Disregarding Unimportant Information
  Noting What Needs to Be Remembered
  Recording Words, Dates, and Figures That Help You Recall Related Information
  Reviewing Notes and Underlining or Highlighting the Most Important Items
  Categorizing Notes in a Logical Order
  Organizing Notes So That Information From Various Sources Can Be Added at a Later Time

Outlining:
  Using Outlining Skills to Write Material That Has Unity and Coherence
  Selecting and Using a System of Notation Such as Roman Numerals
  Deciding Whether to Write Topic Outlines or Sentence Outlines
  Stating Each Topic or Point Clearly
  Using Parallel Structure
  Remembering That Each Section Must Have at Least Two Parts

C. Interviewing and Surveying. Developing and Practicing the Use of:

Identifying the Information Being Sought
Deciding on Appropriate Instrument(s)
Identifying Sources of Existing Instruments
Designing Instruments (e.g., Checklists, Rating Scales, Interview Schedules)
Developing Question Wording Skills (e.g., Factual, Attitudinal, Probing, Follow-up)
Sequencing Questions
Identifying Representative Samples
Field Testing and Revising Instruments
Developing Rapport With Subjects
Preparing a Data-Gathering Matrix and Schedule
Using Follow-up Techniques

Figure 4. Continued.

D. Analyzing and Organizing Data. Developing and Practicing the Use of:
Identifying Types and Sources of Data
Identifying and Developing Data-Gathering Instruments and Techniques
Developing Data-Recording and Coding Techniques
Classifying and Tabulating Data
Preparing Descriptive (Statistical) Summaries of Data (e.g., Percentages, Means, Modes, etc.)
Analyzing Data With Inferential Statistics
Preparing Tables, Graphs, and Diagrams
Drawing Conclusions and Making Generalizations
Writing Up and Reporting Results

IV. USING ADVANCED RESEARCH SKILLS AND REFERENCE MATERIALS

A. Preparing for Type III Investigations
Developing Time Management Skills
Developing a Management Plan
Developing Problem-Finding and Focusing
    Skills
Stating Hypotheses and Research Questions
Identifying Variables

Identifying Human and Material Resources
Selecting an Appropriate Format and
    Reporting Vehicle
Obtaining Feedback and Making Revisions
Identifying Appropriate Outlets and Audiences

B. Media and Reference Skills
Understanding Library Organizational Systems
Using Informational Retrieval Systems
Using Interlibrary Loan Procedures
Understanding the Specialized Types of Information in Reference Books Such as:

Bibliographies	Reviews	Histories and Chronicles
Encyclopedias	Readers' Guides	of Particular Fields or
Dictionaries/Glossaries	Abstracts	Organizations
Annuals	Diaries	Concordances
Handbooks	Books of Quotations,	Data Tables
Directories/Registers	Proverbs, Maxims, and	Digests
Indexes	Familiar Phrases	Surveys
Yearbooks	Source Books	Almanacs
Manuals	Periodicals	Anthologies

Understanding the Specific Types of Information in Nonbook Reference Materials Such as:

Art Prints	Globes	Study Prints
Books on Tape	Maps	Models
Videos	Movie Clips	CDs
DVDs	Pictures	Artifacts
Realia	Slides	
Charts	Films	

Using Electronic Media to Gather Information:

Commercial On-Line	CD-Roms	Video Clips
Services	Chat Rooms	Virtual Tours/Field Trips
Internet/Websites	TED Talks	
E-Mail/Mailing Lists	News Groups	

C. Basic Technology Skills
The Ability to Identify Trustworthy and Useful Information
The Ability to Selectively Manage Overabundant Information
The Ability to Organize, Classify, and Evaluate Information

Figure 4. Continued.

The Ability to Conduct Self-Assessments of Web-Based Information
The Ability to Use Relevant Information to Advance the Quality of One's Work
The Ability to Communicate Information Effectively
See http://edudemic.com/2012/07/10-interactive-lessons-by-google-on-digital-citizenship/ for More Lessons/Skills.

D. Community Resources

Identifying Community Resources Such as:
    Private Businesses and Individuals
    Governmental and Social Service Agencies
    College and University Services and Persons
    Clubs, Hobby and Special Interest Groups
    Professional Societies and Associations
    Senior Citizens Groups
    Art and Theater Groups
    Service Clubs
    Private Individuals
    Museums, Galleries, Science Centers, Places of Special Interest or Function

V. DEVELOPING WRITTEN, ORAL, AND VISUAL COMMUNICATION SKILLS

A. Written Communication

Planning the Written Document (e.g., Subject, Audience, Purpose, Thesis, Tone, Outline, Title)
Choosing Appropriate and Imaginative Words
Developing Paragraphs With Unity, Coherence, and Emphasis
Developing "Technique" (e.g., Metaphor, Comparison, Hyperbole, Personal Experience)
Writing Powerful Introductions and Conclusions
Practicing the Four Basic Forms of Writing (Exposition, Argumentation, Description, and Narration)
Applying the Basic Forms to a Variety of Genre (i.e., Short Stories, Book Reviews, Research Papers, etc.)
Developing Technical Skills (e.g., Proofreading, Editing, Revising, Footnoting, Preparing Bibliographies, Writing Summaries and Abstracts)

B. Oral Communication. Developing and Practicing the Use of:

Organizing Material for an Oral Presentation
Vocal Delivery
Appropriate Gestures, Eye Movement, Facial Expression, and Body Movement
Acceptance of the Ideas and Feelings of Others
Appropriate Words, Quotations, Anecdotes, Personal Experiences, Illustrative Examples, and Relevant Information
Appropriate Use of Audiovisual Materials and Equipment
Obtaining and Evaluating Feedback

C. Visual Communication. Developing Skills in the Preparation of:

Photographic Print Series	Multimedia Images	Videotape Recordings
PowerPoint Presentations	Website Development	
Audio Recordings	Motion Pictures	

Figure 4. Continued.

> › organizing an art festival that features M. C. Escher-like artwork and presenting the display in a local business,
> › creating and publishing a regional poetry journal and submitting it to a national writing competition, or
> › designing a workshop to assist families in investigating their ancestry and reporting the project to a local historical society.

A mentor, teacher, or parent can be instrumental in helping students throughout the development of a Type III project, specifically by assisting in the location of resources, providing background information and feedback, or supplying procedural advice. The teacher's role here is clearly what we like to call "the guide on the side" rather than a disseminator of information. In this regard the teacher serves more as a coach or mentor rather than an instructor.

The more projects a student completes, the better he or she becomes at understanding the process and tapping into human and material resources. Students who are experienced in creative-productivity not only generate better projects over time (Delcourt, 2008; Kay, 1994) but also demonstrate more acute skills at finding problems worth solving (LaBanca, 2008). And research shows that getting ideas or problem finding is the most crucial stage in creative achievement (Csikszentmihalyi, 1999). Sorting through potential ideas to identify those worth pursuing is also the first phase of regulated learning in which students use forethought (Zimmerman, 1998). In addition, highly creative productive students select projects based on the value the topic has to the learner and to a projected audience (Delcourt, 2008). For example, LaBanca (2008) explained that students who are among the highest ranked at the Intel International Science and Engineering Fair (ISEF) are problem solvers who demonstrate high levels of inquiry and are recognized for identifying truly novel problems, rather than for selecting topics that are considered to be merely of technical interest. LaBanca classified science fair projects into four categories: those that provide a review of the literature about a particular topic; technical projects that are used to replicate well-known results, often referred to as "cookbook" projects; technical projects with value that extends the data set and potentially the knowledge base about a known topic; and projects which represent a novel approach to a problem that is of value to the scientific community. Novel approach projects are the goal for students in any realm of study when the outcome is to produce innovative thinking.

Type IIIs—From Start to Finish

Getting started. Choosing something of interest is a key factor in beginning a project. Several researchers have investigated the vital role of problem finding in the problem-solving process (Csikszentmihalyi, 1999; Getzels, 1987; LaBanca, 2008). A key variable is examining multiple possibilities for prospective projects. Therefore, the best advice is to explore many possible ideas before settling on a topic. Being curious and open-minded could lead to a project that is potentially unique and innovative.

Effective use of resources. Resources include equipment, mentors, books, financial support, background information, time, organizational and communication skills, imagination, and appropriate feedback. As individuals work on projects, they learn how to manage their resources and to coordinate their efforts with others to get what they need when they need it. When resources are scarce and students have specific deadlines, their projects might have a limited scope or could be dropped altogether. The inability to access appropriate resources can certainly influence interest in a project; however, the dramatic changes that have taken place in technology and the universal access to the Internet have made access to resources much easier. When giving advice about working on a Type III activity, students have indicated that an early assessment of feasibility is important (Delcourt, 1994.) Fraenkel and Wallen (2003) provided similar advice for those conducting a thesis. They recommended that a topic be feasible, clear, significant, and ethical, prior to investing too much time in the project.

Seeing a project through to completion. What sustains someone to complete a long-range project? Problem-solving tactics, motivation, and the ability to learn from former projects are three important factors that help students to stay on target. Students who work on Type III investigations become expert problem solvers. After locating a topic, expert problem solvers are able to recognize patterns and principles related to their problem, whereas novice problem solvers only see the more obvious and concrete aspects of an issue (Schoenfeld & Herrmann, 1982). This means that expert problem solvers are more adept than novices at understanding inferences that lead to innovative solutions. Experts also break their tasks into manageable parts and are able to use these parts flexibly toward completing an end goal (Larkin, Heller, & Greeno, 1980). Good and Dweck (2005) and Dweck (1986) indicated that those who base their motivation on ways to improve their own learning not only sustain themselves through complex situations, but are more likely to achieve their goals. And we have seen evidence of the highly motivating influence that the "impact on audience" requirement for a bona fide Type III project has in sustaining students' commitments to their work.

Another major influence on creative productive activity is past learning from former projects. In a study of creative productive secondary school students, Delcourt (1993) synthesized the following list based on reports of 18 adolescents who were asked what they learned from working on their creative projects in science and the humanities:

The project itself resulted in
› increased interest and task commitment,
› improved quality of projects completed later,
› the ability to get more ideas,
› better organizational strategies,
› future selection of more challenging projects, and
› the ability to accept criticism more realistically.

Skill acquisition or development occurred in the areas of
› research,
› writing,
› communication, and
› technical abilities.

General personality traits showed improvement in
› self-satisfaction,
› patience,
› self-assurance,
› responsibility,
› attitude toward learning,
› independence,
› enjoyment, and
› passion for a topic (p. 29).

Given the intensity of the activities needed to create the products by Amber and Chris, it is no surprise that they spent considerable time and energy on their investigations. These students need to know their own work styles and to use their time wisely to meet self-established deadlines as well as those imposed by formal organizations, such as science fair committees and publishers.

The role of the audience. It takes someone who is knowledgeable about a topic to provide appropriate feedback. It is also rewarding to present ideas to an appreciative audience. Audience members put an idea into perspective when judging its innovative impact. Certainly, students may need to complete several projects before they understand the process well enough to create products of value, and they can learn a great deal from targeted feedback that can improve their ideas, skills, and final projects.

Barriers. When asked about the criteria related to their least-liked projects, students have referred to barriers related to project completion, such as a lack of commitment and interest; inadequate time, information, and skills for working on a specific project; and poor selection of human and material resources (Delcourt, 1993). In a study of students participating in science fairs, Shore, Delcourt, Syer, and Schapiro (2008) found similar obstacles in the path of project completion, such as lack of time, inappropriate resources, compulsory participation, difficulty in selecting a topic, and lack of support. Research into participation in Type III activities when time and resources are limited should be a topic of future investigations.

Tips to foster innovative behaviors. Although all projects have stumbling blocks, the biggest one is a lack of encouragement. Students need teachers and mentors to guide them in understanding their strengths and interests, to assist them in developing their skills, and to support their creative productive activities. These actions can lead to the development of innovative behaviors, and the following tips can serve as guidelines:

› Teachers have the responsibility to recognize the potential for a child or young adult to be innovative.
› Students should have the opportunities to identify their strengths and learning styles in order to understand how to develop their potential for innovative behaviors.
› Problem finding should be a top priority. Strategies to locate feasible, concise, significant, ethical, and realistic topics should be taught, and enough time should be allocated for this most vital stage of the creative productive process.
› Students who have ideas for making positive changes in their environments should be recognized and encouraged.
› Projects need to be shared with an appropriate audience.
› When students know that they can make significant contributions through their projects, their self-confidence increases, and they are more likely to exhibit these types of behaviors in the future.

› A student's interests need support and guidance, but students need to understand how to work through their problems and projects on their own.

› Barriers that are seen as insurmountable can lead students to prematurely end a project or produce an unethical result. Students should have an outlet to explain their obstacles and have a realistic pathway to complete or exit from a project.

› Students need models of highly effective products in order to see what they can accomplish.

› The developmental nature of creative productive behavior should be recognized. As students practice these activities, they are more likely to become innovative adults.

Continuum of Special Services and Resources

The continuum of special services mentioned in Figure 1 represents a broad range of opportunities and grouping arrangements that a school might provide to meet individual needs. Clubs, service organizations, and extracurricular activities fall into this category. Finally, the resources listed in the right-hand side of the cube in Figure 1 are examples of items that we have developed over the years to make implementation of the SEM easier for teachers and administrators.

Forms of Implementation for the Enrichment Triad Model

Although types of enrichment can be sequenced according to the numbered activities (I, II, and III), they can also be organized around the kinds of experiences in which a student is prepared to engage. This is represented by the flow of the arrows in Figure 3. A student could enter a class with an elementary background about a topic such as botany (Type I), but needs to know how to maintain specific species of plants used for pollination (Type II). Another student might approach a teacher about an idea for a project in photography to be used to illustrate a book (Type III), and needs the time to prepare the book design and layout. Learning should proceed in a natural way from one type of activity to another, as the student's needs change.

The three types of activities can be incorporated into student experiences in a number of ways, which focus on delivering appropriate services to students.

All three types of activities can be implemented within the regular classroom structure or take place in another environment, such as a gifted program, an enrichment cluster, an afterschool program, or a mentorship.

Amber, the student mentioned at the start of the chapter, had difficulty obtaining direct assistance for her interests in physics and astronomy because her local teachers did not have a background in these areas. Her teachers were, however, supportive in making suggestions for resources. She read a great deal on the topic, ultimately turning to works by Stephen Hawking in order to understand the issues related to black holes. She admitted that she was only a novice in this field, but tried to get clarifications for her questions by contacting scientists who were able to supply her with understandable resources and answers to her many questions. Although her science fair project might have been considered only a technical project or a technical project with value, based on LaBanca's (2008) definitions, she continues to study physics, astronomy, and mathematics. Her potential for innovation is still to be discovered.

Chris is another student who has always been interested in science. When he entered a summer program in engineering, he thought he would be building bridges. He never considered the role of a chemical engineer. His experiences in mathematics and in computer technology were practical skills for his assignment in the summer program because he was able to make a useful computer simulation for the cancer growth model. He jumped right into a Type III activity, brushed up on skills where needed, and succeeded in the task. He also completed other projects at his high school. Chris was a member of a pull-out gifted program where he worked either individually or on a team to complete science-related projects. On one occasion, he was a member of a team that wrote a grant to obtain a laser. When Chris's team was awarded the funding, the group built a machine for making holographs and traveled to local and regional schools to demonstrate laser technology.

These are only examples of how students have engaged in activities related to the Enrichment Triad Model. These students also learned how to use resources effectively, harness their own ability to be motivated, and target appropriate audiences for their work. Many students in elementary, middle, and high schools throughout the world participate in programs that use this model to help them develop creative productive activities.

Common Goals and Unique Means

Far too many school improvement models have become so structured and prescriptive that they seldom achieve sustainability. In schools using highly structured approaches, teachers often feel that their professionalism has been taken away from them, that they must essentially follow someone else's "script," and therefore they cannot make creative contributions to what goes on in their own classrooms. Long lists of state-dictated standards, highly structured fill-in-the-blank forms for lesson planning, and endless teacher evaluation rubrics have resulted in a generally disheartened profession and teachers who feel as though they lack any form of ownership in what goes on in their own schools. We have avoided these kinds of structures by establishing three general goals for schools implementing the Schoolwide Enrichment Model (see Figure 5). These three goals all allow teachers the freedom to teach (Renzulli, 2010) by introducing their own creative adaptations to any and all required curricular standards.

The first goal is enjoyment. Anything that we enjoy doing we generally do better, and we tend to grow and try to improve in the process. Enjoyment leads to engagement: a commitment to become intrinsically involved in and energetic about what one is learning or doing. Research has shown that higher engagement results in higher achievement (Dotterer & Lowe, 2011; Greenwood, 1991; Reyes, Brackett, Rivers, White, & Salovey, 2012; Wang & Holcombe, 2010). And engagement leads to enthusiasm for the act of learning itself. We also recommend that the following list of high-end learning objectives be used as a guide for planning all enrichment activities:

> › Plan a task and consider alternatives.
> › Monitor one's understanding and the need for additional information.
> › Identify patterns, relationships, and discrepancies in information.
> › Generate reasonable arguments, explanations, hypotheses, and ideas, using appropriate vocabulary and concepts.
> › Draw comparisons and analogies to other problems.
> › Formulate meaningful questions.
> › Transform factual information into usable knowledge.
> › Rapidly and efficiently access just-in-time information and selectively extract meaning from that information.
> › Extend one's thinking beyond the information given.
> › Detect bias, make comparisons, draw conclusions, and predict outcomes.
> › Apportion time, money, and resources.
> › Apply knowledge and problem-solving strategies to real-world problems.

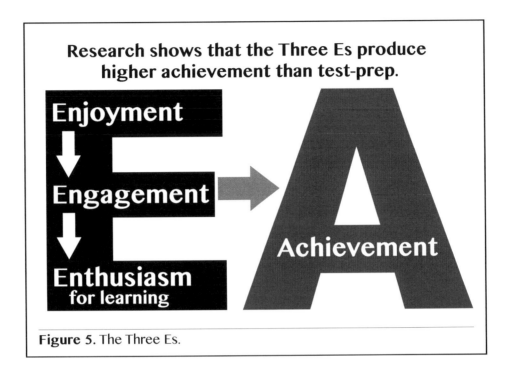

Figure 5. The Three Es.

> › Work effectively with others.
> › Communicate effectively in different genres and formats.
> › Derive enjoyment from active engagement in the act of learning.
> › Creatively solve problems and produce new ideas.

These are the learner-centered skills that grow young minds, promote genuine student engagement, and increase achievement. Although focusing on these outcomes may be counterintuitive to the "more-practice-is-better" pedagogy, we need only look at the track record of compensatory learning models to realize we have been banging our collective heads against walls and following an endless parade of reforms being forced through the schoolhouse door with no results. We need to be courageous enough to explore bolder and more innovative alternatives that will provide all students with a more highly enriched diet—the kind of diet that characterizes learning in the nation's best public and private schools. This is not to say that we should abandon a strong, standards-based curriculum that focuses on basic competencies. We just need to make whatever we are teaching more interesting, engaging, and joyful.

We also need to infuse into the curriculum a series of motivationally rich experiences that promote student engagement, enjoyment, and a genuine enthusiasm for learning. Common sense and our own experience tell us that we always do a better job when we are working on something in which we are personally engaged—something that we are really "into," and that we truly enjoy doing. Take, for example, the demonstrated benefits in performance that result from extracurricular activities that are based on a pedagogy that is the opposite of the pedagogy of drill and practice. How many unengaged students have you seen when students are participating in the math league, the school newspaper staff, the basketball team, the chess club, the debate team, the concert choir, or any other extracurricular activity? Their engagement occurs because these students have some choice in the area in which they will participate, and they interact in a goal-oriented environment with other like-minded students interested in developing expertise in their chosen area. They use authentic problem-solving, interpersonal, and creative strategies in order to produce a product, service, or performance, and their work is brought to bear on one or more intended audiences other than, or at least in addition to, the teacher. The engagement that results from these kinds of experiences exemplifies the best way to approach learning, one that differs completely from the behaviorist theory that guides so much of prescriptive and remedial education.

All learning, from diapers to doctorate, exists on a continuum ranging from deductive, didactic, and prescriptive, on one hand, to inductive, investigative, and inquiry-oriented on the other. Students who have not achieved a certain, predetermined score are subjected to endless amounts of repetitive practice material guided by the didactic model. Then, when scores do not improve, we often think that the obvious solution is to simply redouble our efforts with what has been popularly called a "drill and kill" approach to learning—an approach that has turned many of our schools into joyless places that promote mind-numbing boredom, lack of genuine student and teacher engagement, absenteeism, increased dropout rates, and the other byproducts of overdependence on mechanized learning. Proponents of popular but extremely prescriptive reading programs may boast test scores slightly higher; however, the endless drill and practice only prepare students for more test-taking rather than actually learning to read, enjoying reading, and making reading an important part of their lives.

All Roads Lead to Rome

With these three common goals and the high-end learning objectives in mind, we encourage schools to make their own decisions about how the goals will be achieved. The metaphor that we sometimes use is that "all roads lead to Rome" (in this case, the Three Es). However, there are many ways to get to Rome. We believe that the unique means for "getting to Rome" is based on the selection and use of a program development model that has two essential requirements. First, a model should consist of a shared mission and set of objectives. Everyone (or at the very least, almost everyone) involved in the selection and implementation of a model should agree that the mission and objectives represent a "destination" that they would like to reach. If an agreed-upon goal is "to get to Rome," then there is no ambiguity, vagueness, or misunderstanding about where everyone is going.

This first requirement of a model means that a great deal of front-end time should be spent exploring alternative models, discussing and debating the advantages and disadvantages of various approaches, and examining related factors, such as underlying research, implementation in other schools, and the availability of supportive resources. Reaching consensus before embarking upon a journey will help ensure that everyone involved will get to Rome rather than to Venice or Moscow!

Although we advocate that programs based on the Schoolwide Enrichment Model should strive to accomplish an agreed-upon mission and set of objectives, we also believe that any plan for program development must allow for a great deal of flexibility in the achievement of its objectives. This flexibility is necessary because no written plan or set of procedures can take into account the variations that exist at the local school level. Differences in school populations, financial resources, the availability of persons from the community at large, and a host of other local variables must be considered in the implementation of this or any other approach to school improvement. A model that does not allow for such flexibility could easily become a straightjacket that simply will not work when one or more of the local considerations are not taken into account. Some schools will have supplementary resource teachers for advanced-level students, and others will not. Some school districts will have an abundance of community resources readily available, and others, perhaps more geographically isolated, will have limited access to museums, planetariums, colleges and universities, etc. Some schools may serve larger proportions of culturally diverse students than others, and certain highly selective schools may have such a large number of high-achieving students that they have been designated as schools for the gifted.

Another reason why we believe that a model for program development must maintain a large degree of flexibility is that educators tend to quickly lose interest in "canned" programs and models that do not allow for local initiative, creativity, and teacher input. New and better ways to provide enrichment experiences to students will be discouraged if program development does not encourage local adaptation and innovation to occur. The SEM does provide a certain amount of general direction in both the development of program objectives and in the procedures for pursuing these objectives. At the same time, however, the specific types of activities that educators select and develop for their programs—and the ways in which they make these activities available to various populations of students—will actually result in the creation of their own programming model. Educators will, in effect, be writing their own resource guide based on the activities that they select and develop. We have found that if the three general goals of the Schoolwide Enrichment Model and the high-end learning objectives are maintained, even if in a slightly modified form, a school's program will achieve the integrity that is sought in this total system approach. In this regard, the program that educators develop will attempt to achieve the best of two worlds! First, the program will benefit from the theoretical and research developments and the many years of field-testing and practical application that have led to this particular approach for total talent development. Second, the ideas, resources, innovations, and adaptations that emerge from local situations will contribute to the uniqueness and practicality of programs that are developed to meet local needs. And we have found over the years that many teachers and leaders from excellent SEM schools have contributed to the profession by sharing their work at conferences, workshops, and in various publications. We view this type of sharing as a best-case example of teacher leadership and the extended professionalization of the work of teachers who have achieved the best of both worlds.

In all of our work, we have consistently recommended that educators should make whatever modifications and adaptations are necessary to the particular procedures recommended for accomplishing various program tasks. We believe that there are many pathways and alternatives to reaching desired program outcomes. Once everyone in a school has agreed upon a destination, the uniqueness and excitement of the journey should involve the creation of an individualized plan for getting there. If all roads lead to Rome, what an unimaginative, and indeed, even boring world it would be if there was only one way to get there! Each school develops its own ownership of the SEM by the ways in which it selectively adopts, adapts, and creates the methods, materials, and organizational components that will make the school and program an original application of the Schoolwide Enrichment Model.

Concluding Thoughts

Although we have advocated a larger talent pool than traditionally has been the practice in gifted education, a talent pool that includes students who gain entrance on both test and nontest criteria (Renzulli, 1988), we firmly maintain that the concentration of services necessary for the development of high-level potentials cannot take place without identifying and documenting individual student abilities. Targeting and documenting does not mean that we will simply play the same old game of classifying students as "gifted" or "not gifted," and let it go at that. Rather, targeting and documenting are part of an ongoing process that produces a comprehensive and always evolving "Total Talent Portfolio" about student abilities, interests, and learning styles (Dunn, Dunn, & Price, 1977). The most important thing to keep in mind about this approach is that all information should be used to make individual programming decisions about present and future activities, and about ways in which we can enhance and build upon documented strengths. Documented information will enable us (a) to recommend enrollment in advanced courses or special programs (e.g., summer programs, college courses), and (b) to provide direction in taking extraordinary steps to develop specific interests and resulting projects within topics or subject matter areas of advanced learning potential.

Enrichment specialists (i.e., gifted education teachers) must devote a majority of their time to working directly with talent pool students, and this time should mainly be devoted to facilitating individual and small-group investigations (i.e., Type IIIs). Some of their time with talent pool students can be devoted to stimulating interest in potential Type IIIs through advanced Type I experiences and advanced Type II training that focuses on learning research skills necessary to carry out investigations in various disciplines. To do this, we must encourage more classroom teachers to become involved in talent development both through enrichment opportunities and in curriculum modification and differentiation within their classrooms. We must also encourage more classroom teachers to participate in enrichment teams that work together to provide talent development opportunities for all students in the school, enabling the enrichment specialists to work with more advanced students.

SEM programs must have specialized, trained personnel, who work directly with talent pool students, to teach advanced courses and to coordinate enrichment services in cooperation with a schoolwide enrichment team. The old cliché, "Something that is the responsibility of everyone ends up being the responsibility of no one," has never been more applicable than when it comes to enrichment or gifted education specialists. The demands made upon general education classroom teachers, especially during these times of mainstreaming and heterogeneous grouping, leave precious little time to challenge our most able learners and to accommodate interests that clearly are above and beyond the regular curriculum. A study completed by The National Research Center on the Gifted and Talented (Westberg, 1991) found that in 84% of general education classroom activities, no differentiation was provided for identified high-ability students. Accordingly, time spent in enrichment programs with specialized teachers is even more important for high-potential students.

Related to this nonnegotiable are the issues of teacher selection and training and the scheduling of special program teachers. Providing unusually high levels of challenge requires advanced training in the discipline(s) that one is teaching, in the application of process skills, and in the management and facilitation of individual and small-group investigations. These characteristics of enrichment specialists, rather than the mere grouping of students, have resulted in achievement gains and high levels of creative productivity on the parts of special program students.

Every profession is defined, in part, by its identifiable specializations, according to the task(s) to be accomplished. But specialization means more than the acquisition of particular skills. It also means affiliation with others who share common goals, the promotion of one's field, participation in professional activities, organizations, and research, and contributions to the advancement of the field. It also means the kinds of continued study and growth that make a difference between a job and a career. Now, more than ever, it is essential to fight for the special program positions that are falling prey to budget cuts. All professionals in the field should work for the establishment of standards and specialized certification for enrichment specialists. They should also help parents organize a task force that will be ready at a moment's notice to call in the support of every parent (past as well as present) whose child has been served in a special program.

There may never have been a time when so much debate about what should be taught has existed in American schools. The current emphasis on testing, as connected to federal legislation, the standardization of curriculum, and the drive to increase achievement scores, has produced major changes in education during the last two decades, including the area of mathematics that is our focus in this book. Yet, at the same time, our society continues to need to develop creativity in our students. As overpopulation, disease, war, pollution, and starvation increase both in the U.S. and throughout the rest of the world, the need for creative solutions to these and other problems is clear. The absence of opportunities to develop creativity in all young people, and especially in talented students, is troubling. In the SEM, students are encouraged to become partners in their own education and develop a passion and joy for learning. As students pursue creative enrichment opportunities, they learn to acquire communication skills and to enjoy creative challenges. The SEM provides the opportunity for students to develop their gifts and talents and to begin the process of lifelong learning, culminating, we hope, in creative productive work that they choose.

Enrichment programs have been the true laboratories of our nation's schools because they have presented ideal opportunities for testing new ideas and experimenting with potential solutions to long-standing educational problems. Programs for high-potential students have been an especially fertile place for experimentation because such programs are usually not encumbered by prescribed curriculum guides or traditional methods of instruction. The SEM provides a repertoire of services that can be integrated in such a way so as to create "a rising tide lifts all ships" approach. The model includes a continuum of services, enrichment opportunities, and three distinct services: curriculum modification and differentiation, enrichment opportunities of various types, and opportunities for the development of individual portfolios, including interests, learning styles, product styles, and other information about student strengths. In Chapter 3, we outline surveys to assess interest, instructional styles, and expression styles to help develop individual portfolios in mathematics. Not only has this model been successful in addressing the problem of high-potential students who have been underchallenged, but it also provides additional important learning paths for creative students who achieve academic success in more traditional learning environments but long for opportunities for innovation in school.

When all is said and done, we hope you will agree with a school superintendent who said, "The Schoolwide Enrichment Model is nothing more than organized common sense."

CHAPTER 2

Developing Mathematical Talent in Your Students

The U.S. education system too frequently fails to identify and develop our most talented and motivated students who will become the next generation of innovators. . . .Without properly motivating, encouraging and intellectually challenging gifted students, we may lose some of their mathematical talents forever. (National Council of Supervisors of Mathematics, 2012)

Chances are you picked up this book because you are interested in finding effective strategies and tools to service talented math students in your classroom, school, and/or district. But this begs several questions: Who are students with math talent or high math talent potential? How do we encourage students to develop their potential? How do we ignite the spark to motivate some students to unleash their hidden potential? It all starts with knowing what mathematical talent actually is.

A VIEW FROM THE CLASSROOM

Kayleigh, a third grader, loves looking for patterns whenever she sees a sequence of numbers. She is very fast at determining a general pattern for a number sequence. She loves thinking about and working with really big numbers as well as really small numbers. She asks lots of questions to see if the patterns she finds can be extended to these quantities.

Brendan is a bright ninth grader. He loves geometry and is really good at it. He especially likes working with two- and three-dimensional shapes using computer simulations and software. He can transform a three-dimensional shape in his mind and predict images faster than other students, even when they are using physical models. In his free time, he likes creating building designs and cityscapes and thinks he might like to become an engineer or architect.

Eleven-year-old Sierra often has a really unusual way of approaching challenging problems. She frequently comes up with an idea that her teacher has not even thought of! Her favorite activity is working on independent math projects, and she has just completed a project on exploring different types of fractals found in the world around her.

What Is Math Talent?

If you ask 10 teachers to define mathematical talent, you will probably get a variety of different answers and not just because their students are at different grade levels. The reality is mathematical talent covers a broad spectrum of mathematical understandings.

In the 1960s, Krutetskii, a Russian psychologist, was interested in finding out just what mathematical talent was. So he went to the source, students. Similar to the methods of Piaget, he used observations of many students as they actually worked on math problems. From his studies, he found that students who had high mathematical ability were of three types: those with an "algebraic cast of mind," who reasoned abstractly; those with a "geometric" mind, who had a keen sense of spatial visualization and abilities; and those who had a combination of the two types (Krutetskii, 1968/1976).

This should make sense when you think about your high school math courses. You and/or your friends may have enjoyed more, and performed better in, either algebra or geometry. If you wondered why, you now know! As a high school teacher, math department head, and district math coordinator, I saw many students who loved and did well in one, but not always both, of these subjects. Most recently, my grandson, Skyler, a sixth grader, struggled in his honors math class during the computation chapters but soared when he studied the geometry chapter. His self-confidence in his math ability also soared!

In addition, Krutetskii (1968/1976) found that talented students actually saw the world through a mathematical lens, a "mathematical cast of mind." They think about mathematics in qualitatively different ways. Researchers have found other characteristics common to mathematically gifted students, and you should be on the lookout for these kinds of behaviors in students. They include a focus on conceptual understanding (Sheffield, Bennett, Berriozabal, DeArmond, & Wertheimer, 1999), an ability to abstract and generalize (Krutetskii, 1968/1976; Sriraman, 2002), persistence and ability to make decisions in problem-solving situations (Frensch & Sternberg, 1992; Sriraman, 2003, 2004), and mathematical creativity (Glas, 2002; Sriraman, 2008).

Unfortunately, mathematical creativity is a trait that is often not considered. In fact, the Common Core State Standards for Mathematical Practice (National Governors Association Center for Best Practices [NGA] & Council of Chief State School Officers [CCSSO], 2010) do not even mention it. However, Johnsen and Sheffield (2013) proposed a new mathematical practice encompassing creativity: "Solve problems in novel ways and pose new questions of interest to investigate" (p. 16). A problem that is simply stated can have far-reaching implications in terms of creative solutions. Take, for example, "How many ways can you make 24?" Primary students initially come up with adding or subtracting two numbers such as $12 + 12$ or $30 - 6$. Of course, there is a great variety of ways to do this. They might also extend the operations to multiplication and division, using more than two numbers to compute. Figure 6 is what one student shared when given this task.

This begged the question "Can you find all the ways to make 24 using two numbers and the four operations?" To get all solutions, students need to think about an organized way to list them and look for patterns in doing so. Is there a way to do this? Can you ever list them all? These are fun math ideas to explore, and they encourage students to wonder and marvel at the beauty of mathematics.

The same question can be used to stimulate high-level thinking and use advanced mathematics with gifted students. Depending on their knowledge base and use of resources, they can tap into many areas of mathematics to come up with creative solutions. Figure 7 includes a few solutions that students shared with us. They include exponents, square roots, factorials, mean, Base 2, graphs of functions, triangle angles, and even a Riemann Zeta Function. Wow! Were we impressed! Even more so because of the creativity and use of mathematical

How Many Ways Can I Make 24?

Addition
23+1=24
22+2=24
12+12=24
etc.

Multiplication
6×4=24
8×3=24
12×2=24
etc.

Addition + Sub
20+5-1=24
30-10+4=24
10+10+5-1=24
etc.

Subtraction
25-1=24
34-10=24
124-100=24
etc.

Division
48÷2=24
96÷4=24
etc.

Addition + Subtraction

Addition + Mult.
10+2×7=24
3×10-6=24
4×5+4=24

Mult + Division
6×8÷2=24
12×12÷6=24

Figure 6. Student response to the problem "How many ways can you make 24?"

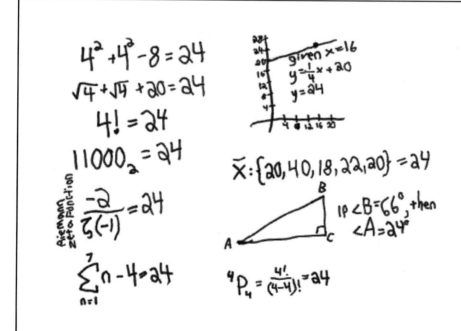

$$4^2+4^2-8=24$$
$$\sqrt{4}+\sqrt{4}+20=24$$
$$4!=24$$
$$11000_2=24$$
$$\frac{-2}{\zeta(-1)}=24$$

Riemann Zeta Function

$$\sum_{n=1}^{7} n-4=24$$

given x=16
$$y=\frac{1}{4}x+20$$
$$y=24$$

$$\bar{x}:\{20,40,18,22,20\}=24$$

If ∠B=66°, then ∠A=24°

$${}^4P_4=\frac{4!}{(4-4)!}=24$$

Figure 7. Student responses to the problem "Can you find all the ways to make 24 using two numbers and the four operations?"

concepts and skills these gifted students employed to come up with these inno-vative solutions.

Sriraman (2008) argued that creativity is a highly desirable, although far from universal, trait in mathematically gifted students that needs to be recog-nized and developed in order to move the field forward. So although you might at times be frustrated by the student who always asks, "I wonder if . . ." and/or goes off in a totally different direction from your math classroom conversation, he or she could be the future mathematician who discovers a new theorem to change the way we view the world! We need to pay attention and nurture creative energy and ideas.

TEACHER TIP!

As educators, it is important to note that Krutetskii (1968/1976) concluded from his extensive observations that neither speed nor facility in computation, nor the ability to memorize formulas, were necessary require-ments for math talent. More recent research has confirmed this finding, recog-nizing that speed in doing mathematics is secondary to mathematical insight (Davidson & Sternberg, 1984; Sowell, Bergwell, Zeigler, & Cartwright, 1990).

Looking for Math Talent in Your Students

In the Schoolwide Enrichment Model, a talent pool of above-average abil-ity/high-potential students is identified through a variety of measures. What does this look like for math? Understanding that math is more than facility with computation and formulas means there is a need to find new ways to iden-tify students with math talent and math talent potential. Schools and districts vary widely on their identification process. Some districts focus on test scores, such as IQ tests, SAT and ACT tests, the EXPLORE test, and standard-ized achievement tests, such as the Iowa Tests of Basic Skills, the Measures of Academic Progress (MAP), and/or district-level tests. Other districts focus on class performance and report card grades. Some use a combination of the above.

Although these can be useful, they should not be the sole identifiers. Be aware of drawbacks with both types of testing. Although ability tests focus on analytical reasoning, they do not measure creative problem solving or problem posing, so some students may be missed. Most standardized and local math assessments focus on skills and procedures, and thus often concentrate on low-level concepts and tasks rather than analytical or creative mathematical thinking. Again, you may miss some students. Finally, some students are just not good test-takers!

A different approach, and one that is consistent with the SEM philosophy, is to look for mathematical behaviors in students that are similar to those of professionals in the field: in this instance, mathematicians. Keep in mind Renzulli's (1978) Three-Ring Conception of Giftedness discussed in Chapter 1 (p. 8). Gifted behavior consists of behaviors that reflect an interaction among three basic clusters of traits: above-average ability, high levels of creativity, and high levels of task commitment. Look for students who are interested in mathematics and have curious and intuitive mathematical minds. They come up with creative ways to solve problems that you may never have considered. They constantly wonder about mathematics: If I laid out one billion pennies, how far would they stretch? What is the smallest possible number? How many sides can a polygon have before it becomes a circle? They love solving challenging math problems and will stick with a problem until they find the answer. And when they do, that "aha moment" is priceless, as evident in their smiling faces and triumphant "Got it!"

In this vein, The National Research Center on the Gifted and Talented developed a Mathematics Scale to help teachers rate behavioral characteristics that were similar to how mathematicians work. This scale is an addition to the Scales for Rating the Behavioral Characteristics of Superior Students (SRBCSS; Renzulli, Smith, White, Callahan, & Hartman, 1976). These scales have undergone several revisions and are still one of the most widely used in gifted education. Unlike many math scales, which are merely a checklist of items put together by educators, the SRBCSS Mathematics Scale underwent rigorous research with content reviews by experts in mathematics and gifted education and a pilot test with teachers who rated more than 726 students in grades 4–6 in urban, suburban, and rural settings. Scores from the scale have strong internal consistency reliability ($\alpha = .98$). There is a teacher-training component that helps insure reliable scores for individual administration (Renzulli, Siegle, Reis, Gavin, & Sytsma Reed, 2009).

These behaviors are also promoted by the National Council of Teachers of Mathematics (NCTM, 2016) as being evidence of students with talent or talent potential:

> Students with exceptional mathematical promise include those who demonstrate patterns of focused interest; are eager to try more difficult problems or extensions or to solve problems in different, creative ways; are particularly good at explaining complex concepts to others or demonstrate in other ways that they understand mathematical material deeply; and/or are strongly interested in the material. (p. 1)

From 2002–2007, we directed a U.S. Department of Education Javits curriculum research grant, Project M³: Mentoring Mathematical Minds, in which we developed curriculum units and conducted a national field test for students with math talent and math talent potential. Using these scales, we developed a student profile in math (see Figure 8) to help teachers identify students for participation in our program. We worked in suburban, urban, and rural schools with culturally and linguistically diverse students from a range of socioeconomic backgrounds. The Student Math Profile includes ratings on behavioral characteristics (the SRBCSS Mathematics Characteristics Scale), as well as teacher evaluation of classroom performance and other existing school assessments. The profiler was instrumental in selecting students who had critical and creative mathematical thinking skills and also enjoyed the subject—in short, the students who were thinking and acting like student mathematicians. These are the students whom you should be looking for. Notice that we asked teachers to rate one-half of the students in their regular math class. We wanted to be inclusive rather than exclusive. Similar to Krutetskii's (1968/1976) methodology, we recommend using classroom observation and interviews with students as they discuss how they work on mathematical problems to help you better complete the scales.

TEACHER TIP!

In order to find behavioral characteristics similar to those used by mathematicians, you need to provide an environment in which students

Project M³ Student Profile

Date: _____ School: _____

Name of Student: _____

Name of Teacher: _____

Instructions: Please complete this form for the top one-half of the students in your class. Read each item in the scale and place an "X" in the box that corresponds with the frequency you have observed the behavior.

Scoring:
  a) Add the total number of X's in each column to obtain the "Column Total."
  b) Multiply the "Column Total" by the "Weight" to obtain the "Weighted Column Total."
  c) Sum the "Weighted Column Totals" across to obtain the Total Score.

MATHEMATICS CHARACTERISTICS[1]
© 2003 M. Katherine Gavin

The student . . .	Never	Very Rarely	Rarely	Occasionally	Frequently	Always
1. is eager to solve challenging math problems (A problem is defined as a task for which the solution is not known in advance).	☐	☐	☐	☐	☐	☐
2. organizes data and information to discover mathematical patterns.	☐	☐	☐	☐	☐	☐
3. enjoys challenging math puzzles, games, and logic problems.	☐	☐	☐	☐	☐	☐
4. understands new math concepts and processes more easily than other students.	☐	☐	☐	☐	☐	☐
5. has creative (unusual and divergent) ways of solving math problems.	☐	☐	☐	☐	☐	☐
6. displays a strong number sense (e.g., makes sense of large and small numbers, estimates easily and appropriately).	☐	☐	☐	☐	☐	☐
7. frequently solves math problems abstractly, without the need for manipulatives or concrete materials	☐	☐	☐	☐	☐	☐
8. looks at the world from a mathematical perspective (e.g., notices spatial relationships, finds math patterns that are not obvious, is curious about quantitative information).	☐	☐	☐	☐	☐	☐
9. when solving a math problem, can switch strategies easily, if appropriate or necessary.	☐	☐	☐	☐	☐	☐
10. regularly uses a variety of representations to explain math concepts (written explanations, pictorial, graphic, equations, etc.).	☐	☐	☐	☐	☐	☐
Add Column Total						
Multiply by Weight	×1	×2	×3	×4	×5	×6
Add Weight Column Totals						

Scale Total ☐

Over ⇨

Figure 8. Project M³ student profile.

Please comment on the student's performance in mathematics.

1) Class Performance (This should include class work, test scores, and/or report card grades. We also encourage you to attach student work samples that show in-depth solutions to a math problem, written responses to open-ended problems, math journal responses, and/or homework.)

2) School-wide or district-wide test scores (Report as percentage such as 91% or as number correct/total number of items such as 42/45. Include DRA or DRP scores if available.)

3) State or national standardized test scores. (Name of test and score. Report score as in #2 above.)

4) Other circumstances or considerations that might influence this student's performance in Project M^3.

Figure 8. Continued.

have a reason to use them. This is not a typical "drill and practice" activity, nor is it procedure-based instruction. It means giving students real, engaging problems that do not have a ready solution or obvious strategy to get to the solution. The struggle is what engages students in the mathematical behaviors that are akin to practicing mathematicians. We will provide examples in Chapters 4 and 5 to demonstrate what we mean.

Looking for Math Talent Potential in Your Students

VIEW FROM THE CLASSROOM

As Principal Investigator of Project M³, I had the opportunity to talk with principals to encourage them to participate in our project. I distinctly remember sitting in the office of a principal in an urban school with a high concentration of low-income students/families. When asked to have his students take part in the study, he said, "I would love to help you, but we don't have any students with math talent in my school." My response was, "How about students with math talent potential?" He quickly stated, "Oh, we have plenty of those students." And so he did. In fact, one of these students, a Latino boy, who participated in our project from third through fifth grade, won a national award in problem solving from NCTM. The principal became a believer in the meaning of developing math talent and actually recruited several other schools in his district to join our team.

In the United States, there are complicating factors in identifying math talent. There are large disparities in individual families' economic means and resources. In addition, there are disparities among schools and districts regarding access to resources and opportunities. Thus, students have varying levels of opportunities of exposure to mathematics at home and school. So a student may have a strong reasoning ability, yet not have been given the opportunity to think about challenging problems to showcase or develop this ability. We have witnessed this time and time again, especially in our work with at-risk students.

In 1994, NCTM established a task force to examine mathematical talent and make recommendations for identification and programming in schools. The task force purposely chose the term "mathematically promising," rather than gifted or talented, to highlight inclusion of students who previously may have been unidentified because of lack of opportunity at home and/or at school to high-level mathematical problems and processes. This definition is compatible with the broadened definition of giftedness that the federal government issued when the Javits Gifted and Talented Students Education Act was passed in 1988.

The task force defined mathematically promising students as "those who have potential to become leaders and problem solvers of the future" (Sheffield et al., 1999, p. 310). They defined mathematical promise

> as a function of ability, motivation, belief, and experience or opportunity. This definition includes the students who have been traditionally identified as gifted, talented, precocious, and so on, and it adds students who have been traditionally excluded from rich mathematical opportunities. This definition acknowledges that students, who are mathematically promising, have a large range of abilities and a continuum of needs that should be met. (p. 310)

In a recent position statement, *Providing Opportunities for Students With Exceptional Mathematical Promise*, NCTM (2016) reiterated its commitment to finding math talent potential across populations:

> Exceptional mathematical promise is evenly distributed across geographic, demographic, and economic boundaries. Growing and leveraging such mathematical promise is essential for our field and society to thrive. (p. 2)

Notice this definition includes motivation, belief, experience, and opportunity in addition to ability. This is not only true for at-risk students but also for all students. If you are not providing a rich, problem-based curriculum that stimulates curiosity and creativity, then motivation and opportunity to use the tools of mathematicians are not available to your students. But we know that experience or opportunity is an even bigger issue with at-risk students. One way we have found to help discover potential in students whose first language is not English, as well as students who have reading difficulties, is to offer a nonverbal ability assessment (Gavin, Casa, Adelson, Carroll, & Sheffield, 2009). In these kinds of assessments, there are no written words. They are composed of figures and/or pictures, and students use analytical and spatial reasoning to determine what comes next in a sequence. In fact, these types of reasoning are ones used by mathematicians in their work. Using these assessments, we were able to identify students that clearly would have been missed using only standardized assessments and teacher recommendations.

VIEW FROM THE CLASSROOM

Ana, a second grader whose family only spoke Spanish at home, was part of our 5-year Javits research study to identify students with math talent potential and field-test math curriculum designed specifically for talented elementary students (Gavin et al., 2009). Ana was identified to participate in the project in third grade based on her 90th percentile score on a nonverbal assessment. She displayed strong math analytical skills! Her teachers were surprised. Their plan was to keep her back to repeat second grade due to her poor reading ability. Reluctantly they agreed to promote her, and she was part of the gifted math program in third grade. She came alive! From barely answering questions in the beginning of third grade, she was an active participant at the end of the year with the highest score on the final math unit test. She went on to continued success in elementary school and studied algebra in eighth grade. We wonder where she would be today if she had not been given this opportunity.

In our national field-test of curriculum designed for talented math students, approximately 50% of the 400 students who participated were students with multiethnic/racial backgrounds from low-income families. Many of these students were like Ana. Our research results (Gavin et al., 2009) demonstrated that these students made statistically significant gains in their mathematical understanding of challenging math concepts. And perhaps most importantly, they learned to love math. Nonverbal ability assessments serve a purpose!

Along with nonverbal assessments and the SRBCSS Mathematics Scale, we also suggest using local norms versus national norms and using measures that indicate opportunities to learn, such as number of years attending U.S. schools, for effective identification of students who are at-risk and/or who are English language learners (ELLs).

Teachers as Math Talent Scouts

In summary, think of your job as a talent scout! And look for talent and to develop talent in your students. Give all of your students a reason to love math and give them a chance to act like mathematicians. Don't view your job as a gatekeeper to the math talent pool, but rather as a recruiter who is looking to offer an extended opportunity to students who love math and exhibit the mathematical behaviors outlined in the SRBCSS Mathematics Scale. You are searching for our future mathematicians, who are vital to making this growing technological and global world a better place in which to live.

Key Points

›   Recognize that math talent is more than computational acuity and memorizing formulas and that there are different types of mathematical talent.
›   Use a variety of measures to identify students, including observation of mathematical behaviors akin to those of practicing mathematicians.
›   In order for students to display these characteristics, provide challenging math problems that require persistence and creativity to arrive at solutions.
›   Search for talent that is hidden within students due to language or other differences. Nonverbal ability assessments can help.
›   Include and look beyond students who demonstrate strong math ability. Think about math talent potential and developing talent in your students.
›   Remember that math talent is not a fixed trait; rather it can grow and be developed in your students.

CHAPTER 3

Math Enrichment Opportunities for All Students— Type I Activities

Every effort must be made in childhood to teach the young to use their own minds.

For one thing is sure: If they don't make up their own minds, someone will do it for them.

—Eleanor Roosevelt, *You Learn By Living*, 1960/2011

Why Provide Enrichment Opportunities in Mathematics?

VIEW FROM THE CLASSROOM

When I am at a social event and people ask me what I do, I tell them I am a math teacher. Inevitably their first response is, "I was never good at math." And then eventually they wander away from the "math nerd" to find someone to whom they can relate better! I often wonder if I said I was a language arts teacher or a social studies teacher, would I get the same reaction? I don't think so.

When I tell this story in professional development workshops, teachers laugh but are definitely not surprised. In fact, I see many nods. I am baffled by the fact that it seems to be acceptable to not be good at math. In fact there is camaraderie in this belief among many adults. When I conference with parents about their child who is struggling in mathematics, they often respond, "Well, I was never good at math, either." Perhaps as a teacher you have had that experience, too.

But this is not true in other societies. I had an opportunity to travel overseas and visit schools in several countries, including Singapore, Japan, Korea, and Hong Kong. When I told teachers and parents my story, they looked at me strangely. Talking with them, I learned that they believe students are just as capable at doing mathematics as they are at reading and writing. It is not surprising to see that the United States is ranked consistently lower than these countries on international mathematics assessments. The 2015 Trends in International Mathematics and Science Study (TIMSS; NCES, 2015) showed Singapore, Korea, Hong Kong, Japan, and China are the top five countries (not necessarily in that order), with students scoring the highest in mathematics in both fourth and eighth grade. These were the same top five countries that had students scoring the highest on the advanced international math benchmark as well. Only 14% of U.S. fourth graders and 10% of eighth graders reached the advanced level, compared to at least half of the Singapore students who participated in the study reaching the advanced level. For older students, the results are still the same. The recent Programme for International Student Assessment (PISA) results (Organisation for Economic Co-Operation and Development, 2016) showed 15-year-olds from these five countries, along with several other countries, outperform their U.S. counterparts.

Why, here in the United States, are we so different in our belief system about learning and understanding mathematics? There is no question that "math anxiety" is a real phenomenon is this country. Parents rarely complain about helping their child at home with reading books or writing stories. But when it comes to math, we often hear, "I never learned it that way, and I can't figure out what is going on. Why can't they just teach it the way I learned it?" This always makes me wonder. If the way we used to teach it does not produce strong math thinkers and good test scores and, moreover, has created a culture of math-anxious adults, why should we continue to teach it the same way?

We need to change this, and change starts with us as teachers. We need to embrace the challenge of instilling confidence in our students so they believe that they can do math and do it well.

TEACHER TIP!

From toddlers on up, parents need support with encouraging their children to look at all of the mathematics in the world around them. Just as they encourage their children to read books and actually read books with them, they need to do math with them. I have found that parents need help in figuring out just what that is. Encourage parents to have conversations with their children. For example, when they go on a trip to the local library, provide ideas to explore with their child. *How many windows do you think there are in the library? Let's count some and see if we find any patterns. Maybe we can figure out how many in all without counting all of them. Look at a bookshelf in the children's section. How many of the smaller books on the table do you think would fit on that shelf? How many of the larger books? How did you figure it out?* It is a matter of being conscious of opportunities to find the mathematics. And it is fun for both parents and children to think about math questions together.

Being Good at Math . . . What Does It Mean?

VIEW FROM THE CLASSROOM

As a math coordinator, I had an opportunity to create and teach an algebra class to a very bright group of 12 seventh-grade students. I was so excited to work with these students! But I soon found to my dismay that some of the students were upset because they did not know the answers to the problems right away. For the first time in their schooling, math was hard and it did not come easily. They thought they were no longer smart in math because it took time to figure out the answer. But isn't this exactly what mathematicians do? They come up with interesting problems to solve and then struggle, sometimes over many years, to find the answers. And they love the struggle! It was hard for me to convince my students that it was natural to struggle with hard problems and that once they found the answer, the reward was so much greater than already knowing the answer to a simple question.

This experience made me realize we needed to start so much earlier than seventh grade in providing interesting and challenging mathematics. We cannot continue to give students questions that are easy to answer to make them feel good. This is an insult to them and their capabilities. Students need to begin using the processes and skills mathematicians use at a very early age, so that they come to embrace the struggle and love hard problems! Being good at math means wanting to solve hard problems and being persistent when solving them. It means being good at posing new problems and trying different ways to solve a problem. It means acting like practicing mathematicians.

You Are Either Good at Math . . . or You're Not!

In our society, not only is it acceptable to not to be good in mathematics, but also there is a pervasive feeling, even among educators, that you are either good at math or you are not. This is far from the truth. The reality is that you can get better at mathematics and, in fact, do get better at it, if you are offered the right opportunities. We have witnessed this in our research over the years working with students from a variety of backgrounds (Casa, Firmender, Gavin, & Carroll, 2017; Gavin et al., 2009; Gavin, Casa, Adelson, & Firmender, 2013; Gavin, Casa, Firmender, & Carroll, 2013).

And you can develop a love for math at any stage in your educational experiences. Think about this. Kindergartners come to school loving math. They love to count, order objects, and sort shapes. They do it for fun, over and over again! And they are good at it. But as early as third grade, research has shown that students have decided that they are either good at math or they are not. How do they come to this conclusion? Is it the way we are teaching mathematics? Is it the kind of mathematics we are teaching? Is it our preconceived notions of what being good at math means and who is good at math? These are questions you need to think about as you plan your math instruction.

A Simple Mantra

We have found it helpful to think about using this simple mantra in teaching: *Each student in my math class needs to learn something new every day.*

Perhaps part of the reason that students begin to dislike mathematics is that they are bored. They already know what is being taught. Using the Early Childhood Longitudinal Study, with a very large participant base of 11,500 students and 2,100 teachers, researchers (Engel, Claessens, & Finch, 2013) found that although the vast majority of children entered kindergarten having mastered basic counting and able to recognize simple geometric shapes, their teachers reported spending the most mathematics time—typically about 13 days per month—on this content. Also, on average, exposure to this basic mathematics content was negatively associated with math achievement across kindergarten. So spending time on material students already knew was essentially a waste of time for them and did not help them do any better on assessments. Many talented math students sit in a classroom in which they already know the material or come to understand it much faster than their peers. They, too, are bored. In fact, Reis and her colleagues (Reis, Westberg, Kulikowich, & Purcell, 1998), in their curriculum compacting research studies, found that mathematically advanced elementary and middle school students were able to have 70%–80% of the regular curriculum eliminated because they already knew it.

Pressure to Perform on High-Stakes Assessment—What to Do?

Every educator is aware that there is pressure to perform on state, national, and international tests from principals, superintendents, parents, and even realtors who are trying to sell homes in the area. This has been heightened in some instances by the connection of student assessment results to teacher evaluation.

But mathematics teaching and learning should never be about "teaching to the test." In fact, districts that drill students over and over with problems similar to the test problems often do not see the test results they anticipate. Students are bored in class and don't see the point of the math they are doing. We need to develop in our students a desire to learn math in order to use it throughout their lifetimes. In just the last 3 months alone, I have met and worked with a number of adults who use math on a regular basis as part of my home renovation project. I marvel at the facility that carpenters, contractors, plumbers, and electricians have with numbers, in particular, fractions that so often are the bane of students and many adults. I worked with architects and designers whose spatial reasoning and use of transformations were second nature. At the same time, I am disappointed at the lack of facility with math that I see at the cashier counter when the computer is not working to provide the correct change. I often need to help the cashier, and I think he or she would believe whatever I said, plausible or not, just to move on to the next customer.

However, studying mathematics is more than learning the content. Studying mathematics is how students learn analytical reasoning skills that are used in every other discipline. They learn how to think logically, how to explain their thinking in an orderly and clearly understood manner, and how to defend their thinking in order to prove an argument. These are life skills that carry over to all disciplines throughout schooling and to life beyond. In math class, students should have a chance to pose new problems and come up with creative solutions to problems. And these behaviors should be the impetus behind the teaching and learning of mathematics.

Student Success Without Drill and Kill Practice

Many teachers feel they can't veer from the traditional curriculum or their students will not perform well on the high-stakes tests. But our research results show students do better on traditional standardized tests (e.g., Iowa Tests of Basic Skills [ITBS]) when they don't spend much time or, in some cases, any time, on the material being tested. In our 6-year U.S. Department of Education Javits Grant project, Project M³: Mentoring Mathematical Minds, we compared students using our math units with students who were equivalent in demographics and ability but used a traditional math program. In our program, students studied above-grade-level content focused on conceptual understanding and learned in line with the way mathematicians work. Students did not spend a lot of time on computation or traditional word problems. However, their performance on the ITBS mathematics section (heavily focused on computation) was statistically superior at each grade level (third, fourth, and fifth) for two different cohorts of students (Gavin et al., 2009). How could this happen? We believe that if students saw something new on the test, they were used to being challenged and could figure it out. The reasoning skills and problem-solving process they had learned helped them, much more than drill and practice on the kinds of problems on the test.

Teachers as Change Agents

So give yourself permission to move away from the standard textbook lessons and let students explore, create, and dig into interesting and challenging mathematics. Create an environment that inspires and engages students, one in which they come to love math.

TEACHER TIP!

I had a great high school teacher who loved math, and it showed. Because of her, I started loving math and enjoying the challenge of interesting and hard problems. She was my change agent, and I went on to major in mathematics and become a middle school and high school mathematics teacher, math department chair, math coordinator, and gifted mathematics education professor. Never underestimate the influence you have as a teacher. It is an awesome gift and an awesome responsibility.

Enrichment Triad to the Rescue: Type I Experiences

So how do you instill this love of mathematics? How do you make mathematics challenging and fun at the same time? This all starts with exposing all of your students to a variety of enrichment experiences.

The Schoolwide Enrichment Model

As mentioned in Chapter 1, at the core of the SEM is the Enrichment Triad Model, which is designed to engage students in learning, engender enjoyment, and spark curiosity to learn more.

In the general SEM, Type I Enrichment is designed to expose students to a variety of topics, careers, hobbies, persons, places, and events across a broad spectrum of disciplines. These experiences are not normally part of the regular curriculum. Usually an enrichment team composed of teachers, parents, and students works together to research topics, contact speakers, set up interest centers, create enrichment clusters, plan field trips, find media and technology resources, etc. This enrichment can be provided for all students or for those students who have expressed an interest in a particular topic or field.

So what do Type I Enrichment experiences look like in math? First of all, we hope you now see the value and need for providing Type I Enrichment experiences for all of your students. And you are probably wondering: How can I do this? Is it going to take too much of my planning time and too much of my teaching time? You need to know that it is definitely worth the effort. You will not only create a lively classroom full of eager learners, but over the long haul you will also see students' understanding of mathematics increase (and your state and district test scores rise!).

Making Plans

We suggest you start small. Take the lead and create a planning team. You can plan on your own, but if you take the time to put together a few interested folks to talk about options and help in the planning, it will really help get the ball rolling. You will appreciate the brainstorming, collective energy, and support a team generates. We suggest contacting the following people:

› the math specialist/coach/department chair and/or district math coordinator,
› the gifted/enrichment specialist/coordinator,
› administrators (principal and/or assistant principal, director of curriculum, etc.),
› fellow math teachers within and/or across grade levels,
› interested parents and students, and
› community members with math interest and expertise.

You may end up with a group of 10 people, or it may be you and one other interested person. Whatever the team looks like, get started.

Type I Math Activities

The activities you plan can and should have a variety of math topics, a variety of different materials, a variety of ways to engage with the materials, and a variety of venues. Your purpose is to show students what mathematics is really all about, who uses math in the real world, and how fascinating it can be. You want them

---

HOW MUCH IS IT WORTH?

The green triangle is worth one point. Find the values of the blue, red, and yellow pieces, using the area of the green triangle as a guide.

- What is the value of a figure made with three triangles, four red pieces, two blue pieces, and one yellow piece?
- Make a design that uses exactly eight pieces and is worth 23 points.
- Make as many figures as you can that have a total of 23 points. Use a chart to list your findings. Find and describe as many patterns as you can.

Figure 9. Sample pattern block center.

---

to end up wanting more . . . wanting to learn more, wanting to do more math, wanting to explore a math topic in more depth. We have categorized Type I Math Activities into three areas of focus: mini-investigations, people, and places.

Mini-Investigations

Mini-investigations are short math activities that promote Renzulli's Three Es (enjoyment, engagement, and enthusiasm), while developing critical and creative mathematical thinking skills. They give students a taste of a particular topic in mathematics using a variety of materials and methods.

Interest centers. One of the easiest ways to introduce mini-investigations to your students is setting up interest centers. Interest centers (which are also learning centers) are a logical extension of the math classroom and can not only create fun, hands-on experiences for your students, but they also can help you observe different math interests of students as well as their preference for how they learn (instructional styles) and ways they like to do math (expression styles). There are a variety of ways to create and use interest centers. Some teachers like to put a bucket of materials, such as LEGOs, pattern blocks, or color tiles, in a center and let students explore by building or creating different designs. They can be encouraged to explore interesting questions using the material. This is a good start, and you may already do this. We encourage you to make sure the probing questions are high level and also leave room for creative explorations. For example, you can build an effective pattern block center with the activity in Figure 9.

Magical math days. You can also set up a series of varied math centers, short focused activities, that take an entire class period and/or extend over a couple of math classes. Vary the math topic, materials used, and ways for students to communicate their findings. Students love this "break" from the routine, and you will find your classroom abuzz with the Three Es. These magical math days are a great way for you to observe your students as mathematicians in action and will help you plan for Type II activities addressed in the next chapter.

VIEW FROM THE CLASSROOM

Monica, a fourth-grade teacher, decided she and her students needed a change. Rather than jump right into the next unit in the math textbook, they needed to come into a math class that was exciting, engaging, and hands-on. She wanted to embrace Type I Enrichment and worked with her grade-level partners and the math specialist in her school to create a series of mini-investigations that students could rotate among to experience a variety of mathematics. She chose number, algebraic thinking, geometry, and measurement as her topic areas and used games, manipulative materials, and computers to appeal to the different instructional and expression styles of her students. She created six mini-investigations (see Figure 10) that allowed students to explore different topics in math focusing on critical and creative thinking and having fun! She encouraged them to work in pairs to brainstorm and play the games. She called these classes "Magical Math Days," and the students loved them. She included some extension activities for students who showed interest in a particular activity and wanted more!

Monica used these centers in two consecutive math classes to allow her students to get involved in the investigations. Her students loved them so much, they asked her to keep them available in the back of the room. One of her teaching partners felt more comfortable setting them up around the room for students to use during their free time, including recess. She was pleasantly surprised to see how many students chose to explore the centers, including multiple visits, rather than go out to play on the playground. Another teacher worked with a parent and created a Family Math Event using the centers. The point is, you can do this in different ways and find a way that will work best for you, your colleagues, and your administrators. We strongly encourage you to give it a try.

OUR MAGICAL MATH DAY

1. **Eggcitement:** How would you measure a fried egg? List at least five different ways. Include what you are measuring, the tools you would use to measure the egg, and how you would do it.

2. **Guess Which Block Is in the Box?** Take a careful look at each of these blocks. (*Note.* Monica displayed the blocks that she borrowed from the Kindergarten teachers shown in the photo below.)

   Another block just like one of these is inside the box. Without opening the box, can you and a friend guess which one it is? You must agree on your choice. Then, write down three reasons for your guess.

   Creative Extension: Design a 3-D figure different from the ones shown that would fit in the box.

3. **Build What I've Created:** (*Note.* Monica had two identical sets of Cuisenaire rods [you could use other shapes of varying sizes and/or lengths] and a divider to block viewing, such as a file folder, at this center. Each student takes a packet of rods.)

   Working with a partner, choose who will be the first "builder." Put the divider (barrier) between you and your partner.

   Using all of the rods, the builder makes a design or structure that the partner cannot see. When you have finished your building, give oral instructions to your partner to help him or her recreate your design. Partners may ask to have directions repeated. No other questions are allowed! You may only look at your own design.

   Remove the barrier when your partner has completed his or her design. Compare the two structures. How are they alike? How are they different? Write

Figure 10. Sample magical math day centers.

down any key words in the directions that helped you build correctly. What words were confusing to you?

Now switch roles and repeat the activity.

4. **Fun at the Zoo:** In the sentences below, the same animal symbols have the same value. Find the values of each symbol.

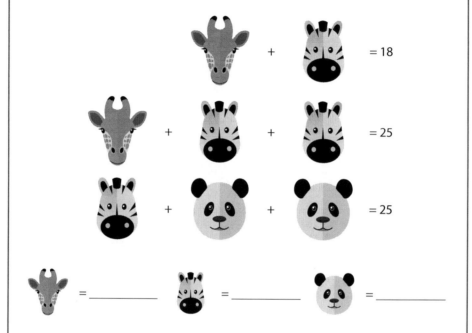

Note. If some students need a hint, suggest that they substitute 18 for the total value of giraffe and zebra in the second equation.

5. **Krypto on the Computer:** (*Note.* Monica set up a computer station with the Krypto interactive from the Illuminations website [see https://illuminations. nctm.org/Activity.aspx?id=3569]. In this interactive game, students are asked to combine five number cards using the four arithmetic operations (+, −, ×, ÷) to reach a target number. This interactive activity uses only the numbers 1–10, and multiple solutions are possible. Monica included a handout of reflection questions at the station for students to think, talk, and write about as they play.)

Which cards are easy to use? Why? Which cards are harder to use? Why? Is there more than one way to reach a particular target number?

Figure 10. Continued.

6. **Question, Please!** At the park playground, there are two sets of swings with four swings in each set. There are three slides and five sets of seesaws. Jamie was thinking of a question about the playground equipment and said her answer was $\frac{3}{4}$. What might her question be?

Here are some other answers about the equipment. What might the question be?

$$\frac{1}{3} \qquad\qquad 12 \qquad\qquad 20$$

Creative Extensions: (1) Create another answer and ask a friend to make up a question that would work for that answer. (2) Create a new puzzle that does not involve the playground.

Figure 10. Continued.

Although we usually think of center activities as part of the elementary classroom, why not consider centers with older students? Imagine your seventh-grade math students or high school algebra students entering your classroom to see it set up with several tables with interesting materials on them and questions to explore that are different at each table. Students love to get up, circulate, and work on different and challenging short activities. What a nice change of pace for your students. I have done this with high school students, and they loved looking at mathematics in different ways. You will be surprised at the positive response, the energy in your classroom, and the way students work on the activities. You can let students choose the centers they visit with the encouragement to try something that is new and different for them. Some sample investigations for older students are included in Figure 11.

Math Trails. Math Trails are another type of mini-investigation. Math Trails have been in existence for many years, beginning in England and Australia. With the advent of the NCTM Standards in 1989, many U.S. educators started creating trails, including a Math Trail around the Boston Commons and Public Gardens and The Mall in Washington, DC. There is a good deal of information about creating trails on the Internet. Here is one site to take a look at that spans the grades and will get your creative juices flowing: http://www.comap.com/highschool/projects/mathtrails/MathTrails.pdf.

These activities show students firsthand how math is connected to the real world, the world that is right around them. For Math Trails, you create a series of mini-investigations that students explore as they walk within the school building, on school grounds, or close by. Besides your school area, you can create Math Trails for a local park, zoo, shopping mall, supermarket, and more. These "trails" create a sense of adventure as students become math detectives and discover that

WEIGHING IN

In the pictures below, the same shapes have the same weights. Different shapes have different weights.

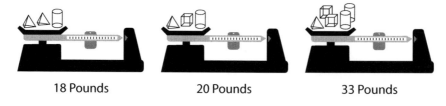

| 18 Pounds | 20 Pounds | 33 Pounds |

△ = ____ pounds   ⬭ = ____ pounds   ⬜ = ____ pounds

NUMBER LINE INTRIGUE

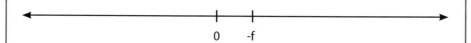

0   -f

1. Write down two things you know about -f from looking at the number line.
2. Now tell me two things you don't know about -f.
3. Place the following numbers on the number line:
    $$2f, -f +2, -f -2, -3f, -g \text{ if } f < g < 0$$

Creative Extension: Which of the numbers that you placed on the number line can be located exactly by using simple geometric constructions?

PAPER PATTERNS

Take an $8\frac{1}{2}$ in. by 11 in. piece of paper and fold it in half. Count and record the number of regions after the fold. If the area of the entire sheet is 1, record the area of the smallest region created by the fold. Continue folding and recording and fill in the following chart, making predictions when needed. Then, complete the graphs and describe what they look like. What interesting patterns did you find?

Figure 11. Sample investigations for older students.

Number of Folds	Number of Regions	Area of Smallest Region
0	1	1
1		
2		
3		
4		
5		
6		
10		
N		

Number of Regions vs. Number of Folds

Area of Smallest Region vs. Number of Folds

Figure 11. Continued.

math is all around them. Your job is to create the activities and provide a Math Trail Map, which is a guide for students to follow as they walk from place to place to discuss and solve interesting problems. You can even create Math Trails for families to do together at home or at a Family Math Event. It is fun to create an "I am a Math Trail Blazer" badge as a reward for everyone who completes the trail.

VIEW FROM THE CLASSROOM

Tom, a seventh-grade math teacher, decided to create a Math Trail for his class. We have listed a couple of activities that he created in Figure 12. Activities like this can get you started creating a Math Trail relevant to your students and your community.

OUR MATH TRAILS

FIRST STOP—THE OLD MAPLE TREE IN THE FRONT OF OUR SCHOOL

1. How wide is our maple tree? Get a group of your friends and hold your arms out, hands touching each other, until you get all of the way around it. Ask each friend to tell you how tall he or she is. Record the heights, and add them together. This is the circumference of the tree. Why is that? (*Hint*: Find out about the relationship of your wingspan [arms extended] to your height.)
2. Now that you know the circumference, you can use a formula you have learned to find the width of the tree. Brainstorm how to do this!

NEXT STOP—THE ELEMENTARY SCHOOL PLAYGROUND NEXT DOOR

3. What is the slope of the slide? Did you ever notice that playground slides don't go straight down. There is always a slope—sometimes gentle, sometimes with curves, sometimes steep. *Slope* is actually a mathematical term that indicates the rate of change in a linear function. The slope of a line is a ratio and is found by dividing the change in the vertical distance by the change in the horizontal distance between any two points. This ratio is always the same for a straight line. The greater the ratio, the steeper the slope. Talk with your partner and decide how you can find the slope of the playground slide. (*Hint*: The vertical distance is the height of the slide at a particular point.)
4. Pick two specific spots on the slide. Measure the distance between these spots. Then measure the height of the slide at these two spots. Then find the slope or ratio of the change in the height divided by the change in the horizontal distance.
5. Now find the slope between a point at the top of the slide and one at the bottom of the slide. Did you get the same slope? Can you figure out why or why not?
6. Try another slide on the playground. Predict if the slope will be greater or smaller than the one you found. See if your prediction is correct.
7. Why do you think the creators of the slide used these slopes? Make a prediction and then research the production of playground slides to find out.

Figure 12. Sample math trails activities.

TEACHER TIP!

Don't underestimate the power of these Type I experiences! Hone your observation skills as you watch students at work on mini-investigations at the interest centers, walking the Math Trail, and being field trip detectives. Observe who gravitates to which activity, who stays the longest, and who repeats an activity. Listen to the questions students ask each other and the kinds of discussion they enter into in your classroom debriefing. You will learn a lot about their math interests, their reasoning skills, their creativity, and their math ability in particular areas. This is a great way to spot math talent and math talent potential in your students. It will be helpful in creating a talent pool to participate in Type II activities and in determining what Type II and Type III mathematics investigations will appeal to your students.

Online mini-investigations. In addition to the above investigations, here are a few of our favorite enrichment websites for individual or small-group investigations that will offer your students a taste of new and engaging math topics at no charge:

› NRICH (http://nrich.maths.org) offers free enrichment activities for students in grades 1–12. Students can select from individual problem-solving activities, such as arranging fences to make the largest rectangular space possible; games to play with a partner, like tug-of-war on a number line by adding, subtracting, multiplying, or dividing numbers rolled on a die; and small-group investigations, such as helping teammates find matching fraction representations without speaking. Instructions and printables are provided for each activity. Some activities are designated as "live" and students are invited to send in their solutions. A selection of solutions is published online.

› NCTM's Illuminations (https://illuminations.nctm.org) offers games, interactive activities, including apps, and brainteasers for students in grades Pre-K through 12. Students can duel Okta the octopus to be the first player to find cards with a specified sum, explore algebraic thinking using an interactive pan balance to determine the value of unknown shapes, and play Krypto (see Figure 10). The site can be searched by grade level, mathematical topic, or activity type.

› Hour of Code (https://code.org) offers engaging one-hour tutorials in coding for all grade levels. Students can design arcade games and apps, create animations or geometric designs, make music, and more, all while being introduced to coding. This can easily lead to further Type II and Type III enrichment on computer coding.

People Resources

Speaker presentations. There is nothing like a person who is in love with his or her job to get students excited about a subject. Brainstorm with your planning team to find local professionals who use math on a regular basis. Invite them to come in and speak with your students. We have found it is most effective if they can do a demonstration or, even better, get students involved in an activity related to their field. Then, students become mathematicians and can experience the power and joy of the subject. Presenters in fields relating to mathematics might include:

› actuaries,
› mathematics and statistics faculty from a local university,
› architects,
› physicists,
› engineers,
› astronauts,
› chemists,
› financial planners,
› bankers,
› small business owners in your community,
› doctors and nurses,
› athletic trainers (Yes, athletic trainers! You might be surprised at how much math they use!),
› builders, carpenters, plumbers, and electricians … and the list goes on …

Multiply Your Options conferences. One particularly effective way to introduce students to a variety of math fields is to organize a conference in which several professionals present short workshops for students to engage in activities that they do in their work. We have hosted these annually at the University of Connecticut in cooperation with school districts to raise interest in STEM-related fields for middle and high school girls. CAMPY (The Connecticut Association for Mathematically Precocious Youth) hosts similar one-day conferences around Connecticut for students interested in mathematics. It is heartening to witness the enthusiasm of the professionals who work with the students and even more heart-warming to see the Three Es explode in each of the sessions. In short, it is a fantastic experience for all involved. Here is a description of activities from three past sessions to help you imagine the possibilities:

› *I Missed You Nearly*: Students design car stunts and test them to gather information about a variety of motions.

› *The Mathematics of Games and Doodling*: Students learn how chaos can produce beautiful patterns, along with a few strategies to win at the game of their choice.

› *STEM for the Win! Sports, Ciphers, and Space With TI-Nspire Technology*: Students compete in a virtual triathlon to understand work, energy, and power; then crack a cryptography code; and finally explore rates of change to get a spacecraft off the ground.

Online video clips. There are some websites that provide excellent video clips on how professionals in the real world use mathematics. Here are a few we find engaging for students.

› The Futures Channel (http://thefutureschannel.com) has excellent short video clips of professionals in a variety of fields using mathematics. Students can see how a skateboard designer uses math in building the perfect board. They can hear a landscape architect discuss how planning park gardens and green space involves lots of mathematics and many, many more professionals. These are great to show at the start of a lesson on a math topic that coordinates with the video and/or if a student expresses an interest in a particular area of mathematics or a particular career field.

› TEDEd Lessons Worth Sharing (http://ed.ted.com/series/math-in-real-life) presents a series of interesting clips on math in real life, from cutting a cake, to posing and solving problems, to interviews. For example, in one TEDEd Lesson (http://ed.ted.com/lessons/pixar-the-math-behind-the-movies-tony-derose), Tony DeRose from Pixar describes the mathematics behind the animation, including how arithmetic, geometry, and trigonometry are used to bring favorite characters to life.

› The Mathematical Sciences Research Institute has created a website, Numberphile (http://www.numberphile.com), with videos of mathematicians talking about their interest in mathematics and discussing problems and ideas in mathematics that drive their passion and are sure to stimulate your students' interest.

Films. There are some powerful films that focus on mathematicians in very relevant and real scenarios to which students can connect. For example, *Hidden Figures* features three African American women mathematicians who were instrumental in launching the space program (and received no credit at the time). Some other favorites include *Stand and Deliver, A Beautiful Mind, The Man Who Knew Infinity, A Brilliant Young Mind,* and *Gifted.*

Books. Biographies of famous mathematicians help students understand that mathematicians are real people and so they, too, can become mathematicians. Here are some to consider.

› *The Boy Who Loved Math: The Improbable Life of Paul Erdos* (2013), written by Deborah Heiligman, tells the story of the Hungarian mathematician who traveled the world collaborating with other mathematicians through simple text and illustrations.
› *Hidden Figures: The American Dream and the Untold Story of the Black Women Mathematicians Who Helped Win the Space Race* (2016) by Margot Lee Shetterly tells the story of Black female mathematicians at NASA whose work helped launch rockets and astronauts into space.
› In *Significant Figures: The Lives and Work of Great Mathematicians* (2017), mathematician Ian Stewart examines the lives of 25 great mathematicians through mini-biographies, including Muhammad ibn Musa al-Khwarizmi, the creator of algebra, and Augusta Ada King, the first computer programmer.
› *Mathematician and Computer Scientist Grace Hopper: STEM Trailblazer Bios* (2016) by Andrea Pelleschi details the life of Grace Hopper from childhood, when she enjoyed taking apart alarm clocks to learn how they worked, through adulthood, when she joined the Naval Reserves during World War II and worked on the world's first large-scale computer.

In addition, here are two websites that provide biographies of mathematicians:
› The School of Mathematics and Statistics at the University of St. Andrews in Scotland (http://www-groups.dcs.st-and.ac.uk/history/BiogIndex.html) has an extensive list of mathematicians with their biographies.
› The Biographies of Women Mathematicians (https://www.agnesscott.edu/lriddle/women/women.htm) website is part of an ongoing project

at Agnes Scott College in Atlanta, GA, to document the achievements of women in mathematics and contains biographical essays on numerous women mathematicians, both historical and current.

Places as Resources

Taking a field trip is often students' most memorable event of the school year. Why? It is truly experiential learning, often hands-on and fun! There are many places of business that showcase mathematics (e.g. science labs, banks, The New York Stock Exchange). There are numerous science museums, discovery centers, and children's museums around the country that have lots of mathematics to uncover. There is also a special museum devoted entirely to mathematics, The National Museum of Mathematics (https://momath.org) in New York City. This museum has several interactive exhibits, including a circular ride on a square tricycle. It also features traveling exhibits that go around the country. So if you are not able to visit New York, look for and/or advocate for Math Midway 2 Go (MM2GO; http://mathmidway.org/mm2go) to come to your area.

There is also an exciting traveling exhibit called MathAlive! (http://mathalive.com/about-the-exhibit) created in collaboration with NCTM, NASA, MATHCOUNTS, the National Society of Professional Engineers, and the Society of Women Engineers. It was launched at the Smithsonian Institution and is now traveling to museums throughout the country. Designed for families and students, the exhibition brings to life the real math behind what kids love most—video games, sports, fashion, music, robotics, and more. Check out when it is coming to a museum near you on its website.

Virtual field trips. The advancement of technology provides us with so many opportunities. One of these is experiencing museum and field trip settings online. Although not quite the same experience as actually being there, it allows students to get a glimpse at outstanding museums around the country that they would never be able to visit in person. Here are some of our favorites:

› The Exploratorium in San Francisco (https://www.exploratorium.edu/explore) has a collection of online mathematical experiences for virtual visitors, housed in the "explore" section of the website. Students can explore graphing and angles by building a seesaw for their smartphone, create geometric art with soap film, and more. The website also includes a large video collection related to exhibits and events at the Exploratorium, blogs about what is happening behind the scenes at the museum, and suggested apps and websites for further exploration.

› On the Smithsonian website (https://www.si.edu), students can explore featured collections, stories, videos, and more related to their interests. There are photographs and descriptions of exhibitions past and present related to math, such as *Slates, Slide Rules, and Software: Teaching Math in America*. Students can watch videos like the math of prehistoric climate change and the math used to create *Harry Potter, The Pop-Up Book*, as well as read math-related stories and articles.

› The Franklin Institute (https://www.fi.edu) in Philadelphia is dedicated to educating about science and technology and continuing Benjamin Franklin's legacy of lifelong learning. The website includes detailed information about all of the exhibits, including photographs and videos. Students can tour features, such as the *SportsZone*, where visitors investigate how momentum and timing affect the height of their vertical jumps, or *Your Brain*, where visitors explore brain science. Temporary exhibits, such as *A Mirror Maze: Numbers in Nature*, are also featured on the site. The Franklin Institute Mobile App, which is downloadable from the museum's website, provides access to a library of virtual reality experiences related to the exhibits, from the deep sea to the flight deck of a space shuttle.

The Math Begins When the Game Ends

In our math curriculum work over the last 15 years, we lived by the phrase, "the math begins when the game ends." It is important to follow up on the Type I exploration students have experienced. A debriefing with the whole class, small groups of students, or an individual student will help you in planning additional Type I, as well as Type II and Type III activities, for students who share a common interest. The idea of providing Type I experiences is to "stimulate new interests that might lead to follow-up by students who share a common interest" (Renzulli & Reis, 2014, p. 119). Invite a speaker to stay and meet with students who have questions and have expressed an interest in learning more. Conduct a debriefing discussion with students to share their problem-solving methods in the mini-investigations, to talk about what math discoveries might have surprised them on the Math Trails, and to find out what they want to know more about. Provide a Field Trip Detective Survey for students visiting museums to give them a focus for their activities and debrief when back in class. These debriefings encourage engaging math discussions and probe more deeply into the specific content or math field in which the students have experienced a brief encounter.

Your planning team should also take time to evaluate the Type I experiences provided. Using teacher observations and student feedback, the team should determine which activities worked well to stimulate enjoyment, engagement, and enthusiasm and which might need some tweaking. Documentation of this evaluation process is also helpful in providing rationale for continuing this important work. Note that evaluation forms for general Type I activities can be found in *The Schoolwide Enrichment Model* (3rd ed.; Renzulli & Reis, 2014, pp. 121–125). These forms can be easily adapted to Type I Math Enrichment Experiences.

Math Interests, Instructional Styles, and Expression Styles Inventories

Along with observation and debriefing with your students, it is important to explore what your students like to learn about and how they learn best. What better way to do this than to ask them? We have created student surveys in three areas to help you get to know your students better. The Math Interest Survey (Handout 1) is especially helpful in determining what type of math activities and what kinds of materials and methods will engage students, stimulate their curiosity, and help them develop what Renzulli has characterized as a romance with the discipline (Knobel & Shaughnessey, 2002). The Instructional Styles Survey (Handout 2) will help you learn how students prefer to learn during a lesson. Learning becomes heightened when students are given an opportunity, at least some of the time, to use their preferred method. You will notice that many of these methods are the varied ways in which mathematicians do math.

Finally, the Expression Styles Survey (Handout 3) helps you learn how students prefer to tell about what they have learned. This is important to consider to keep students motivated and engaged in learning. Provide some opportunities to allow students to choose their style in explaining their ideas or solution to you and/or the class. They will enjoy it more, generally put forth more effort, and hence produce a better product.

Name: _____   Date: _____

SEM-Mathematics Interest Survey

1. Below is a list of labels for tables, indicating the type of math activities available at the table. Which tables would you visit? Mark your first, second, and third choices.

   _____ Numbers, Numbers, Everywhere   _____ Take a Chance on Probability

   _____ Awesome Algebra in the Making   _____ Geometry Is All Around Us

   _____ Data: Collect It, Analyze It, Graph It   _____ Measuring Madness

2. Imagine you are a famous author of a popular math book. What would it be about?

   _____

   _____

3. What title would you give the book?

   _____

4. There are many different topics in math. Think about what you like to do in math. Check the box that describes how much you like or dislike the topic listed.

Topic	Really Dislike	Dislike	Not Sure	Like	Really Like
Computation*					
Fractions					
Decimals					
Percents					
Other number systems					
Really big and really small numbers					
Shapes and space					
Angles					
Measurement (for example: length, area, perimeter, volume)					
Probability					
Data collection and analysis					
Algebra					
Other (name topic):					

*adding, subtracting, multiplying, and dividing whole numbers

Name: _____   Date: _____

HANDOUT 2

SEM-Mathematics Instructional Styles Survey

Think about the ways you like to learn in math and what types of activities you like to do in math class. Check the box that describes how much you like or dislike the certain kind of activity in math.

Activity	Really Dislike	Dislike	Not Sure	Like	Really Like
Do mental math.					
Do calculations with pencil and paper.					
Use the calculator to perform calculations.					
Estimate answers.					
Listen to the teacher explain something in math class.					
Read how to do something in my math book.					
Do a math activity where I use math materials.					
Work with a partner on an activity.					
Play a math game.					
Do a math activity on the computer.					
Talk about math with a partner.					
Have a class discussion about math.					
Build or design a model with blocks or shapes.					
Look for patterns.					
Solve math puzzles and mazes.					
Work on a hard problem.					

Name: _____   Date: _____

SEM-Mathematics Expression Styles Survey

When you are learning something or solving a problem in math class, you usually tell about your ideas or how you solved a problem. Check the box that describes how much you like or dislike expressing yourself in a certain way in math class.

Ways to Express Yourself	Really Dislike	Dislike	Not Sure	Like	Really Like
Talk about my ideas/solutions with a partner.					
Present my ideas/solutions to the whole class.					
Write about my ideas/solutions by myself.					
Write about my ideas/solutions with a partner.					
Use a table or chart.					
Use a Venn diagram or concept map.					
Use a graph.					
Draw a picture.					
Use the computer to share my ideas/solutions.					

CHAPTER 4

Developing Type II Processes and Skills in Mathematics

It isn't enough just to learn—one must learn how to learn, how to learn without classrooms, without teachers, without textbooks. Learn, in short, how to think and analyze and decide and discover and create.

—Michael Bassis, President Emeritus, Westminster College (as cited in Moursund & Sylwester, 2013)

What Do Type II Processes and Skills Look Like in Math?

Developing Type II processes in mathematics means learning and working like a mathematician. This is often far from what a typical math classroom looks like. Often we see the teacher standing in the front of the room, using the math textbook as a guide, and writing on the whiteboard or using a projector or document camera to show students how to do an example. However, this is not how mathematicians work, and this is not how students should be learning mathematics. As we have stated in Chapter 2, learning mathematics is all about the productive struggle. It is not learning how to do something somebody has already figured out. Rather it is about figuring it out for yourself. That is the fun part of math!

When the Common Core State Standards were introduced in mathematics, we were very excited. Why? It was the Standards for Mathematical Practice that caught our attention. These were exactly what we were promoting in our gifted math curriculum programs and what mathematicians do in their work! Let's take a look at them (NGA & CCSSO, 2010):

1. Make sense of problems and persevere in solving them.
2. Reason abstractly and quantitatively.
3. Construct viable arguments and critique the reasoning of others.
4. Model with mathematics.
5. Use appropriate tools strategically.
6. Attend to precision.
7. Look for and make use of structure.
8. Look for and express regularity in repeated reasoning. (pp. 6–8)

These are certainly not new. They are very similar to the Process Standards NCTM emphasized in its 1989 and 2000 Standards. In fact, they are the methods mathematicians use in their daily work—when they are trying to prove a theorem, when they are creating a math model to show how a machine works, when they are developing actuarial formulas, and when they are creating programs for computer games. In short, they use these processes and skills when they do mathematics. We want our students to do the same.

Building on these practices, there is one more very important addition needed. In *Using the Common Core State Standards for Mathematics With Gifted and Advanced Learners*, Johnsen and Sheffield (2013) advocated for a ninth standard, "Solve problems in novel ways and pose new mathematical questions of interest to investigate" (p. 16). What was missing from the Common Core Math Practices? Creativity! The Standards for Mathematical Practice included very important critical thinking skills but left out one of the most important practices that distinguish mathematicians, the ability to create new mathematics.

We also realized that it is students who need to use these practices, and so they need to know what they are. The Common Core State Standards were written for teachers, so the practices were written using adult language. The reality is that teachers need to share these practices and then work with students on developing their abilities to use them on a regular basis when they do math. For students to use the practices, they need to make sense of them. And so we transformed the practices into kid-friendly language for students who use our Projects M^2 and M^3 curriculum units. Students are then conscious of the practices and learn how to use them when doing activities and writing about their thinking in their Student Mathematician's Journals. We encourage you to share these with students, post them in your classroom, talk about how to use them, and point out when students are using them to solve problems (see Figure 13).

The "How-to" Strategies

It is easy to list the nine math practices, but how do you develop them in your students? We have found the practices need to be embedded within the content of the lesson you are teaching or the investigation students are exploring. They are processes, not content, and so students use them when solving problems, explaining ideas, and making sense of the mathematics they are doing. First, you must have the right content—real mathematical problems that are challenging and interesting for students. We will talk more about that in the next chapter. Next, you need to help students use and develop these processes. We have found certain teaching strategies to be very useful in developing these skills in all students and especially in students with math talent who take a real shine to them.

Classroom Discussions

Mathematical communication plays a big part in the development of mathematical processes and skills. Creating a community of math learners provides students with a place to use these practices, and your job is to establish and facilitate such a community. Rather than a classroom where students are working individually on worksheets or textbook pages, no matter how difficult the problems are, we believe students need to talk about mathematics in order to learn and use these processes. The sharing of ideas also stimulates interest, heightens problem solving, and increases learning. For the past 15 years, in our curriculum research projects (Projects M^3 and M^2), our teachers have been using "talk moves." With her colleagues at Boston University, Dr. Suzanne Chapin, one of our author team, created these moves and has done extensive research on their effectiveness (see Chapin, O'Connor, & Anderson, 2013). These talk moves have made such a difference in the level of conversation and student understanding that principals tell us they know when they walk into an M^3 classroom, without even looking at the material students are using. The quality of the interactions between teacher and students and among students is decidedly different, as it is at a more advanced and deeper level. In fact, one principal asked us to come in

THINKING LIKE A MATHEMATICIAN*

Here is a list of skills mathematicians use every day. See how many you can use in your Student Mathematician's Journal.

1. Make sense of problems and keep trying until you solve them.

2. Understand quantities, their relationships, and how to represent them.

3. Build logical reasons to defend your thinking. Consider the reasoning of others and ask useful questions to help make sense of the reasoning. Explain why you agree or disagree with another's reasoning.

4. Use the math you know to help solve problems in everyday life. Use physical models, drawings, tables, graphs, and/or equations to help you.

5. Choose and use the appropriate math tools to help solve each problem.

6. Communicate explanations clearly using correct math vocabulary and symbols.

7. Look closely and use patterns to help solve problems.

8. Notice if you are using the same math again and again and look for short cuts.

9. Solve a problem in a new way. Ask new questions to investigate.**

* Adapted from the Common Core State Standards: Standards for Mathematical Practice

National Governors Association Center for Best Practices (NGA Center), Council of Chief State School Officers (CCSSO). (2010). *Common Core State Standards for Mathematics.* Washington, DC: Retrieved from http://www.corestandards.org/the-standards.

** Johnsen, S. K., & Sheffield, L. J. (Eds.). (2013). *Using the common core state standards for mathematics with gifted and advanced learners.* Waco, TX : Prufrock Press.

Project M³: MoLi Stone   Organization of the Unit   **27**

Copyright © Kendall Hunt Publishing Company

Figure 13. Thinking like a mathematician. From *Project M³: Unraveling the Mystery of the MoLi Stone: Exploring Place Value and Numeration* (p. 27), by M. K. Gavin, S. H. Chapin, J. Dailey, & L. J. Sheffield, 2015, Dubuque, IA: Kendall Hunt. Copyright 2015 by Kendall Hunt. Reprinted with permission.

and train his entire middle school faculty so that the whole school would use these moves.

From our work with teachers and students, we have learned that it matters what teachers say and how teachers say it in order to promote productive talk within the classroom. Teachers are the facilitators and play a very important part in helping students construct meaning, explain their reasoning, justify their thinking, and pose creative questions and problems.

As teacher educators and student teacher supervisors, we always encouraged our preservice and inservice teachers to write down specific high-level questions to ask during a lesson. However, once the lesson was in progress, we found that often notes were put aside and the teacher went with the flow of the lesson, forgetting to include the questions. In post-observation interviews, we often discussed why the teacher never posed the questions. But we all know as educators how easy it is to stray from our original lesson plans. These talk moves provide a framework to be used in all lessons and are based on five simple questions that stimulate the type of productive discussion student mathematicians should be having. You will recognize these moves. You were probably introduced to them in your preservice teacher education classes. However, in packaging them together and bringing them to the forefront of each class discussion, you will witness a classroom filled with curiosity, critical thinking, and creativity no matter what grade level or ability level of students you are teaching. Six talk moves are described below.

Revoicing. The first talk move is called *revoicing*. With this move, the teacher restates a student's idea in his or her own words and then asks the student if the revoicing is accurate. This can help the teacher (and the other students) understand a somewhat unclear statement, or it can emphasize an excellent idea or understanding that was just stated. It also helps the student speaker clarify his or her thinking as the teacher says it aloud again. For example, a teacher might interject in a conversation, "Charlene, I think you are saying that division is the opposite of multiplication. Did I understand you correctly?"

Repeat/rephrase. The second talk move is *repeat/rephrase*. This is similar to the first move except that instead of the teacher repeating what was said, another student repeats or rephrases what was just stated. This validates the speaker's idea and also gives the class a different version of the same idea to ponder. It helps students engage with each other's thinking and reasoning and encourages the entire group of students to get involved in the discussion.

TEACHER TIP!

These first two moves slow down the flow of the conversation and take a while. Don't let that dissuade you! Students gain a much deeper understanding when they are all involved in the discussion and when they hear the same concept presented more than once and in a variety of ways. *One note of caution.* Make sure you choose to repeat or have your students repeat an important math idea. Having them elaborate on how to multiply a three-digit number by a three-digit number is not appropriate. Focus your discussions on mathematical concepts (e.g., understanding the relationship between multiplication and division) rather than on rote procedures. We also encourage you to talk about misconceptions that you want to dispel. Ask students to repeat an incorrect idea that many students may also be thinking. For example, "Maria, can you repeat again for us why you think squares are not rectangles?" Then discuss this as a class to make sure students come to understand the concept correctly.

Agree/disagree and why. The next move is *agree/disagree and why.* This is used when an important math concept is being discussed and a student has put forth an interesting idea, whether correct or incorrect. Teachers should encourage students to think about the idea and then react. This gives the teacher the opportunity to hear how students are processing the idea presented and what they think about it. It actually helps students clarify their own thinking by stating it aloud.

You might be asking, "Why should I belabor an incorrect answer or idea?" One reason is that there may be other students who have the same idea. Another reason is the opportunity to have a rich discussion on a variety of ideas. The most important part of this move is the "why?" This is not a poll of "thumbs up or thumbs down" on who agrees or disagrees with the idea. Rather, the meat of the discussion is the reasoning for agreeing or disagreeing. This talk move should be the heart and soul of the math discussion. It increases the challenge and encourages students to become proficient in the mathematical practices, particularly making sense of problems, understanding quantities, and building logical reasons to defend their thinking and critique the reasoning of others.

Partner talk. Hand-in-hand with this move, is what Chapin et al. (2013) called "Partner Talk." Students turn and talk with a partner about the problem before the class discussion. This allows students to air their ideas with someone else and results in them not only clarifying their ideas but also being more willing to share with the class. Partner talk is used frequently throughout classroom discussions and also affords you the opportunity to observe and listen to many different students as you wander among the pairs while they are talking. Talented math students love to engage with this talk move.

As an example, we witnessed the following discussion between partners in a fifth-grade classroom. They had been thinking about the following scenario: *Jody had tossed a fair coin six times, and each time it came up heads. What are the chances it would come up heads on the seventh toss?* Ellie and Olivia were engaged in partner talk:

> **Ellie:** I think it will come up tails since the probability for heads and tails is equal, and there already have been six heads, so it is bound to come up tails.
>
> **Olivia:** I think either one, heads or tails, can turn up. I think each time the coin is tossed it has the same chance for heads as tails. I think it was just luck that heads always turned up.
>
> **Teacher:** I want you to think about what we said about each individual time we toss a coin. What is the likelihood that it will turn up heads? Tails? Does the coin have a brain that tells it "I think I need to land tails next time"?

If done correctly in a respectful environment, you may hear what we have heard from our M³ students at the end of a discussion, "Now, I disagree with myself!" They have listened to their peers and have been swayed to change their reasoning.

Add on. *Add on* is another talk move used to increase the level and depth of understanding of mathematics concepts, as well as to add creative ideas and new problems to investigate. If a student puts forth the germ of an idea, the teacher asks students if anyone would like to add on to what was said. This helps the original idea become more comprehensive as new perspectives are considered. This also draws more students into the conversation by asking them to add their thoughts to what has been said. Again, this talk move is very popular with talented students who are always eager to share their new ideas. For example, in one class discussion, Charlene, a third grader, stated that division is the opposite of multiplication. The teacher then asked, "Can someone add on to what Charlene just said?" She wanted students to further this idea by explaining the relationship between multiplication and division, an important concept.

Think time. The last move is surely one we as teachers are all aware of, but often neglect, *wait time*. We like to call it *think time*. Mathematicians don't instantly know the answer. The harder and more complex the problem, the more think time they need before formulating a response. Give your students this time. So many of our students who are eager contributors have their hands up to be called upon immediately. Let them think about an idea first by themselves, then talk it over with a partner, and then share their thoughts.

You can also call on a student and then allow some think time if he or she does not respond immediately. If necessary, suggest that you come back later to get a response. And, make sure that you do! Asking another student to respond to the same question can help. It should be easy for the student who needed more time to repeat what was just said. And often the reluctant speaker will now have a better understanding and be able to state his or her own thoughts along with repeating what was said.

It is important to note that, for many English language learners, the talk moves are very helpful. These students often require more repetition to make sense of the language around the ideas. Research has shown that more frequent use of oral language to express ideas results in increased proficiency (Saunders & Goldenberg, 2010). Using the talk moves helps English language learners not only understand the mathematics more deeply but also improve their facility with English.

TEACHER TIP!

For many talented students, discussion is their forte. They love to tell the teacher and the class their ideas. However, it is the teacher orchestrating a productive discussion that encourages them to hone their critical and creative thinking skills that will help them gain the skills that mathematicians use in their daily work. That is why the teacher is critical as the facilitator of classroom discussions.

Writing in Math Class

Mathematicians not only talk about problems and solutions, but also write their thoughts and solutions down for others to read and ponder. Teaching students to be like mathematicians requires them to write down their ideas and explain their thinking clearly, logically, and completely. Helping students acquire this ability can be challenging. They usually have not had the opportunity to write in math class. However, with the advent of new assessments aligned with the Common Core State Standards, more writing is required. So, not only is writing in math a critical skill to becoming a mathematician, but it is also integral to many state requirements.

In our research, we have found that students may have an insightful discussion of a math concept or problem but then are unable to produce writing to mirror their thinking. Again, teachers need to help students develop this skill that mathematicians use so well. To facilitate this, we created graphic organizers to help teachers outline the discussion for students prior to writing about it. Teachers can use the steps below to record on the whiteboard or in a space that is visible to all students:

1. Have students rephrase the question to put it in their own words.
2. Use bullet points to capture ideas presented by a variety of students. Include some misconceptions if they come up, so that all ideas are valued. (This leads to a rich discussion.)
3. Come to a consensus about the response and summarize briefly.
4. Students write about it!

Figure 14 features a graphic organizer template to record this information.

Teachers were concerned that having this outline of ideas on the board would encourage students to just copy down what was there without processing the information and sharing their own ideas. But this doesn't happen! Instead, it helps students solidify their thinking, and they then can write about the question in a clear and logical manner.

VIEW FROM THE CLASSROOM

Tonya, a teacher, and her fourth-grade math enrichment class were discussing the following question as a wrap-up of activities on

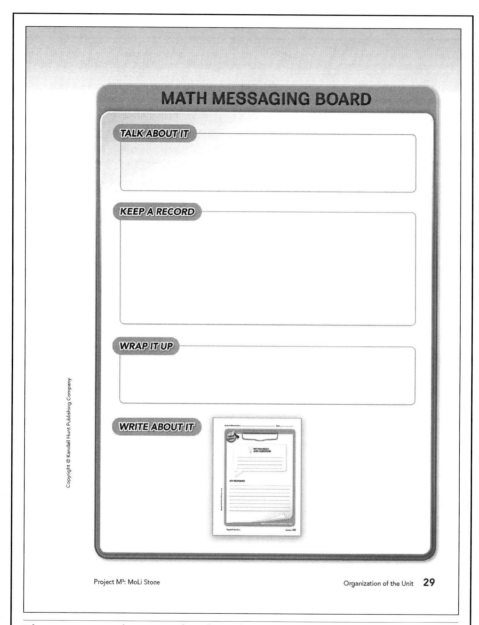

Figure 14. Math messaging board. From *Project M³: Unraveling the Mystery of the MoLi Stone: Exploring Place Value and Numeration* (p. 29), by M. K. Gavin, S. H. Chapin, J. Dailey, & L. J. Sheffield, 2015, Dubuque, IA: Kendall Hunt. Copyright 2015 by Kendall Hunt. Reprinted with permission.

two-dimensional shapes: *Miranda has made a discovery. She claims that all squares are rectangles! Do you agree or disagree? Explain your answer.*

Note that this is an interesting question. Many adults often disagree because the familiar shapes of squares and rectangles look different. But mathematically a square fits the definition of a rectangle, and so it is also a rectangle.

Tonya wrote an outline of the class discussion on the board.

1. **Talk About It:** Can a square also be a rectangle? Why or why not?
2. **Keep a Record:** (This is a brief record of different student comments)
   a. No, a rectangle has two long sides and two short sides. A square has all sides the same.
   b. Yes, a rectangle has right angles and opposite sides of equal length. So does a square.
   c. Can a square be a rectangle but a rectangle not be a square? I know some rectangles are not squares.
   d. A square has opposite sides parallel and equal. So can it be a parallelogram, too? I am getting confused about all the different names for shapes.

3. **Wrap It Up:** A square is a rectangle, but a rectangle is not always a square.

Figure 15 shows one student's written response, which demonstrates how working with students on honing their writing skills is well worth it. As an aside, we presented this writing in a workshop to the math department faculty at the University of Connecticut. The department chair was considerably impressed and said he wished his calculus students would come up with such a clear and complete argument in their work!

Besides using a graphic organizer to record the conversation, we have found that paying specific attention to the mathematical writing process is important. Here are some recommendations that our teachers use to help students succeed:

› Initially, work with students to create an exemplary response to a question, prior to asking them to write on their own for future questions. They need to see what good mathematical writing looks like.
› For some students, working with a partner to create a response is helpful. Discussing how to put their thoughts in writing helps some students who get "writer's block" when they see the paper in front of them.
› One of the most useful (and fun) ways for students to learn how to write is to critique a work sample. Choose a student sample or create one that

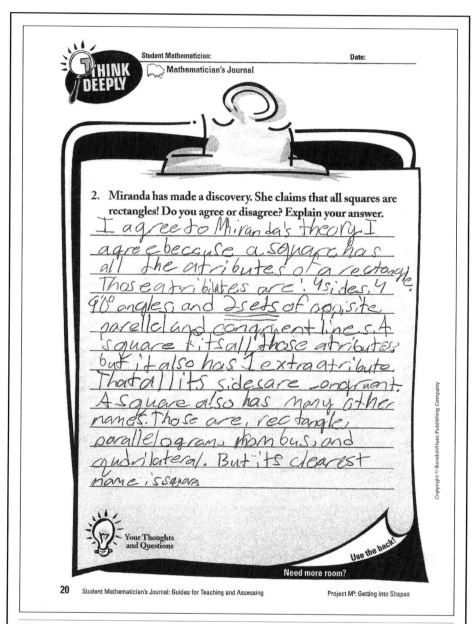

Figure 15. Fourth grader's student mathematician's journal response. From *Project M³: Level 4: Getting Into Shapes Student Mathematician's Journal* (p. 20), by M. K. Gavin, J. Dailey, S. H. Chapin, and L. J. Sheffield, 2015, Dubuque, IA: Kendall Hunt. Copyright 2015 by Kendall Hunt. Reprinted with permission.

has common errors or missing information in it. For example, when asked to find the length of the pencil in Figure 16, Chip, a first grader, wrote that the answer was 5 inches because that was where the point of the pencil ended on the ruler.

Many young students often think this is the case, so discussing Chip's response and how to correct it helped them clarify their thinking. We have found critiquing a writing sample to be the most beneficial in helping students improve their writing in terms of clarity, completeness, and logical thinking.

› We ask students to write in a Student Mathematician's Journal, as shown in Figure 15. This gives them a specific place to keep their notes, write their thoughts and creative ideas, and defend their reasoning. It is exactly what mathematicians do. We often tell them that some of the most profound theorems and proofs were found in the notes in the sidebar of mathematicians' journals. We encourage them to feel free to write about all of their ideas. On the flip side, you need to provide feedback on student writing. Students need to feel that their thoughts and their reasoning are being paid attention to by you, their teacher. You need to take time to value their input and give feedback to help them improve their reasoning and their writing. This is an opportunity for you to see how each student is learning on an individual basis. We know that providing feedback to each entry for each student is so time-consuming that it can be overwhelming. We suggest that you scatter your review of journal writing so that you do a few at a time. Students don't need immediate feedback on everything they write, but they do need feedback from you to show you care and that you are dialoguing with them in a mathematical conversation.

We have found that by using the talk moves to carry on a productive mathematical discussion and by using our writing strategies to support students with communicating their mathematical understandings, students develop the Type II processes and skills that mathematicians use. They truly become student mathematicians.

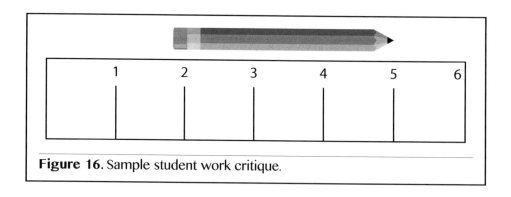

Figure 16. Sample student work critique.

CHAPTER 5

Type II Enrichment in Action

We cannot assume that our Nation's most talented students will succeed on their own. Instead, we must offer coordinated, proactive, sustained formal and informal interventions to develop their abilities. Students should learn at a pace, depth, and breadth commensurate with their talents and interests and in a fashion that elicits engagement, intellectual curiosity, and creative problem solving—essential skills for future innovation. (National Science Board, 2010, p. 2)

As we illustrated in Chapter 4, developing the Type II processes and skills that mathematicians use goes hand-in-hand with developing oral and written skills. It is also important to provide rich and challenging content in order to develop these skills. This is in line with the Type II Matrix (Renzulli & Dai, 2001) that lists cognitive thinking skills as part of Type II Enrichment. These skills include: creative thinking skills; analytic, problem-solving, and decision-making skills; and critical and logical thinking skills. In fact, these skills should be the heart and soul of your mathematics curriculum.

There are several ways in which Type II experiences can develop:

1. They can develop based on students' interests. These interests can emerge as an outgrowth of a Type I experience or from examining their interest surveys or simply from a conversation with a student or a group of students.

2. They can also result from a need to learn new information/content or math skills as part of a Type III investigation.

3. Type II experiences can also be planned in advance, particularly when there is new mathematical knowledge that you would like to share with students or new experiences that will take them beyond the regular mathematics curriculum to challenge and excite them. Sometimes students have no idea of what lies beyond the basic math curriculum, and you can provide an entry into a whole new realm of exploration for them. Your passions and interests can also be a driving force in helping decide these Type II experiences. We all know that when a teacher loves the topic being studied, that enthusiasm often transfers to her or his students.

There are also different environments in which to host Type II Enrichment. You may be the teacher of a self-contained gifted or honors mathematics class. Or you may be the gifted specialist who provides enrichment opportunities for small groups of students. Enrichment clusters and afterschool and summer math clubs/programs are also ideal places to engage in Type II activities. Finally, as a classroom teacher, you can offer Type II Enrichment to all of your students some of the time and some of your students more of the time. Teaching mathematics should always involve teaching the Type II processes and skills that we mentioned in Chapter 4. The CCSS Mathematical Practices, along with the addition of what Johnsen and Sheffield (2013) labeled the ninth mathematical practice ("Solve problems in novel ways and pose new mathematical questions of interest to investigate" [p. 16]), should be a purposeful part of math teaching and learning. All students should learn how to use strategies when doing mathematics. For students who have developed a special interest in a particular topic and/or have shown mathematical talent at the next level, using these skills and processes in connection with advanced and challenging mathematics will provide rich Type II and Type III experiences.

We have found that the most difficult part of teaching Type II processes and skills in mathematics is finding the appropriate math content. Teaching rules to add, subtract, multiply, and divide whole numbers or fractions or integers is not a Type II enrichment experience! In this chapter we provide some examples of mathematical investigations to give you an idea of the kind of high-level mathematics that fosters development of Type II skills and processes and will prepare your students for taking on more independent Type III activities—the highest level of creative productivity in SEM. These are not "enrichment worksheets" you will find in your regular math text. We have found that what is usually listed as enrichment in a standard math textbook is not nearly challenging enough. It is often not advanced material and/or requires very little new learning or effort on the part of the student. Nor are Type II activities math mind benders or puzzles. Although these are fun, and talented students often enjoy doing them, they do not involve exploring a mathematics topic in-depth as mathematicians would.

Instead, Type II activities pose rich problems requiring both critical and creative thinking leading to a much deeper understanding of the math. All of the investigations require students to grapple with a challenging and intriguing problem, discuss and write about their thinking, and justify their answers. This is truly how mathematicians work. Coupled with that, these activities provide students with the Three Es (enjoyment, engagement, and a genuine enthusiasm for learning.)

Primary Level Type II Enrichment

VIEW FROM THE CLASSROOM

Juanita, a first-grade classroom teacher, found that her students got excited about all kinds of shapes. They liked looking for shapes on the playground and had fun making artwork using shapes of different sizes and colors. She decided she wanted to enhance teaching and learning about shapes in their math curriculum. She substituted a unit on shapes designed to help students think deeply about the properties of shapes for her regular geometry curriculum unit. What a difference! She learned that her students were capable of so much more than she had ever expected, and she had fun learning some new things along with them.

To give you an idea of what this Type II enrichment unit looked like, we describe one activity. *Exploring Shape Games: Geometry With Imi and Zani* (Gavin, Casa, Chapin, Copley, & Sheffield, 2011) is a unit from the National Science Foundation Project M²: Mentoring Young Mathematicians. This advanced curriculum for primary students requires them to describe the properties of shapes and see the relationships among different shapes. This is very different from the typical geometry lessons at the primary level. In fact, when we asked kindergarten and first- and second-grade teachers to describe their math curriculum about shapes, it was interesting to hear their responses. Kindergarten teachers told us that they taught students to associate the names of shapes (triangle, square, rectangle, and circle) with their pictures. First-grade teachers said exactly the same thing. And even second-grade teachers iterated the same thing with the addition of hexagon and octagon and a few three-dimensional shapes. With so much repetition, it is no wonder students are bored! Our Type II investigations in this unit go much deeper than this traditional approach.

In *Exploring Shape Games*, students help to create games for Imi and Zani, their bird friends from the Amazon, who are developing these games for children all over the world. In this particular activity, students use a set of label cards and a set of attribute shapes. There are four shapes (circles, squares, triangles, and hexagons). Each type of shape comes in three different colors (white, black, and gray) and two different sizes (big and little.) The attribute label cards are shown in Figure 17.

Students take turns putting labels on intersecting loops and then filling the loops with the appropriate shapes. Figure 18 shows one of the Venn diagrams Juanita developed with her class as the activity got underway.

As we have stated earlier, our motto is, "the math begins when the game ends." We find that the rich discussion and writing opportunities that follow the game, where students can discuss strategies, talk about the purpose of the game, and delve deeply into the mathematics behind the game, is where their Type II skills and processes are put to work in a big way. After playing the game, students were given a "Think Deeply" question to write about (see Figure 19). This particular question focuses on the big mathematical ideas of the unit and is intended to have students grapple with classifying and sorting shapes using the sophisticated representation of a three-loop Venn diagram. Writing about the mathematics and being asked to justify their reasoning advance students' understanding through reflection on their own ideas, a high-level metacognitive skill that is part of a mathematician's repertoire. Putting thoughts into writing is a step above and beyond verbalizing thinking. It focuses on analytical thinking as students work on writing a logical argument. It helps them solidify their understanding and develops appropriate use of mathematical vocabulary. Justifying their thinking also encourages them to make explicit their understanding of the mathematics. These are all Type II skills and processes and part of the CCSS Mathematical Practices, or how to think and act like mathematicians.

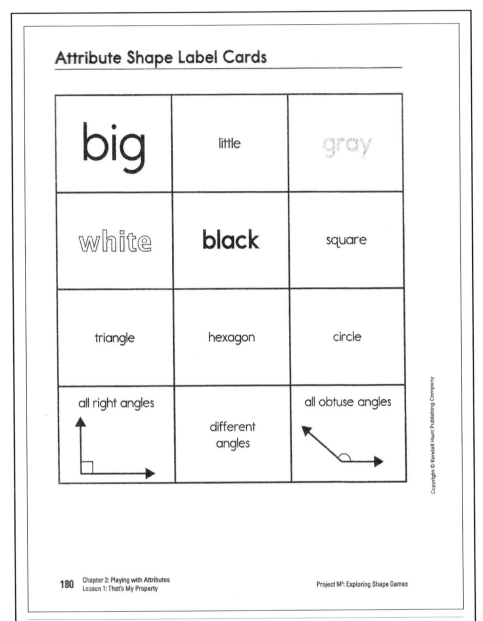

Figure 17. Attribute shape label cards. From *Project M²: Level 1, Unit 1: Exploring Shape Games: Geometry With Imi and Zani Teacher Guide* (p. 180), by M. K. Gavin, T. M. Casa, S. Chapin, J. V. Copley, and L. J. Sheffield, 2011, Dubuque, IA: Kendall Hunt. Copyright 2011 by Kendall Hunt. Reprinted with permission.

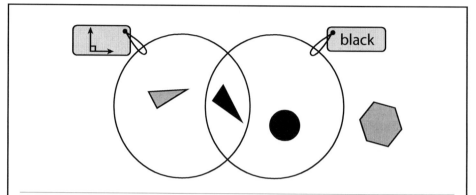

Figure 18. Sample Venn diagrams. From: *Project M²: Level 1, Unit 1: Exploring Shape Games: Geometry With Imi and Zani Teacher Guide* (p. 136), by M. K. Gavin, T. M. Casa, S. H. Chapin, J. V. Copley, and L. J. Sheffield, 2009, Storrs: University of Connecticut, Neag Center for Gifted Education and Talent Development. Copyright 2009 by Neag Center for Gifted Education and Talent Development.

Remember, we said Juanita was substituting this unit for her whole class. The units in Project M²: Mentoring Young Mathematicians were designed for all primary students. But we wrote these from a different perspective. Rather than writing curriculum for students "in the middle" in terms of ability and then trying to differentiate for more advanced students and for students who need more help, we wrote our curriculum units from an advanced perspective. Then we provided more supports for students who might need some math background or more exposure to a particular concept. We found this raised the level of instruction and learning for all students, and students rose to the challenge. For those exceptional students, there are also "Think Beyond" cards, a sample of which is found in Figure 20.

For more information on Project M² materials, see the resource section on page 151.

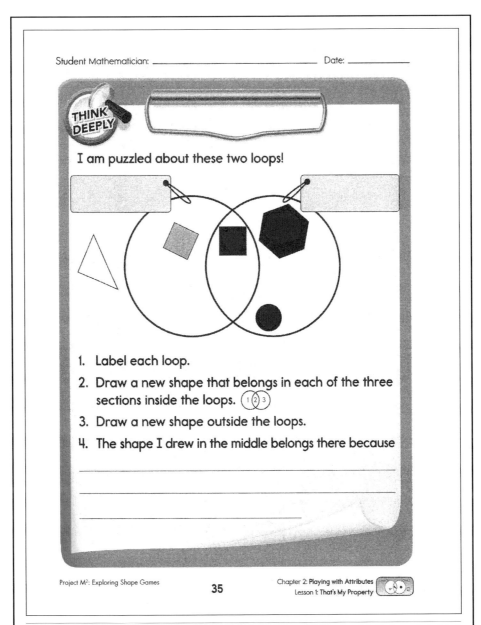

Figure 19. Sample Think Deeply question. From *Project M²: Level 1, Unit 1: Exploring Shape Games: Geometry With Imi and Zani Teacher Guide* (p. 35), by M. K. Gavin, T. M. Casa, S. H. Chapin, J. V. Copley, and L. J. Sheffield, 2011, Dubuque, IA: Kendall Hunt. Copyright 2011 by Kendall Hunt. Reprinted with permission.

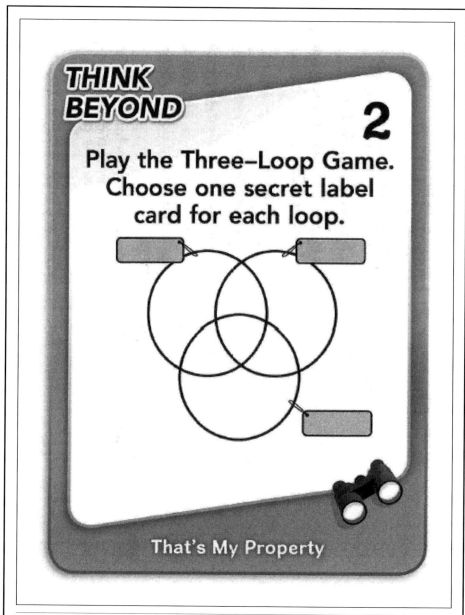

Figure 20. Think Beyond card. From *Project M²: Level 1, Unit 1: Exploring Shape Games: Geometry With Imi and Zani Teacher Guide* (p. 183), by M. K. Gavin, T. M. Casa, S. H. Chapin, & L. J. Sheffield, 2011. Dubuque, IA: Kendall Hunt. Copyright 2011 by Kendall Hunt. Reprinted with permission.

Elementary Level Type II Enrichment

VIEW FROM THE CLASSROOM

Derek is a gifted enrichment specialist who has a grade 5 pullout program for mathematically talented students. His job is to provide math enrichment to these students who also participate in the general classroom math instruction. One day his students came in talking about games they were playing at an indoor recess session. They were flipping a coin to see who went first. Mariah and Samya had done this six times—and "heads" won each time. So Samya figured that because there was supposed to be an equal chance that "tails" would appear, she would choose "tails" next. But "heads" came up again! They thought the coin was a trick coin, but it wasn't. They wanted to know how this could possibly happen—that heads would appear seven times in a row with the flip of a fair coin.

Derek felt this was a perfect opportunity for his students to explore some probability in more depth. They had done many small experiments with probability in math class over the years but had never gone much beyond playing the games. Students became excited when he asked them if they wanted to study a unit called *What Are Your Chances? Probability in Action* (Gavin, Chapin, Sheffield, & Dailey, 2015).

The unit Derek chose was from our U.S. Department of Education Javits research grant project series, Project M³: Mentoring Mathematical Minds, designed specifically for mathematically talented elementary students. In *What Are Your Chances?* students learn about the likelihood of events, the Law of Large Numbers, experimental and theoretical probability, and fair and unfair games based on probability. These are advanced topics for elementary students, and Derek knew they would not be duplicating any material in their regular math program.

The "Odd or Even" game is an example of one investigation from this probability unit. In this game, two players must spin two spinners and find the sum of the two numbers they land on. If the sum is odd, one player gets a point. The other player gets a point if the sum is even. First, students are asked to predict if the game is fair by just looking at spinners similar to the ones in Figure 21.

Derek asked his students if they thought the game was fair. They had lots of opinions! Jordan thought it was fair because you got to take turns. Carrie thought it was unfair because there are four numbers on one spinner and only three on the other. Samya had a different reason. She thought it might be unfair because there are four even numbers and only three odd numbers. Asking students to weigh in on the fairness ahead of time encourages them to analyze the situation and, in effect, act like mathematicians. It also increases excitement in seeing the outcome.

Next, students played the game in pairs, spinning 16 times. They collected class data and again discussed the fairness of the game. Remember, "the math begins when the game ends." They used the results of their experiment to calculate experimental probabilities, and they considered the Law of Large Numbers. Finally, they realized they needed to find all possible sums and see if there was an equally likely chance to get an even sum and an odd sum (i.e., theoretical probability) in order to determine fairness.

Once they determined that the game was indeed fair, they were given a "Think Deeply" question to discuss and then write about (Gavin, Chapin, Sheffield, & Dailey, 2015): "How could you change the rules of the game 'Odd or Even,' keeping the spinners the same, to make it unfair? Using probability, explain why the change makes the game unfair" (p. 178). After finishing the lessons in the unit, the students became very excited about the culminating project, creating a Carnival of Chance to raise money for a charity of their choice. They chose their local pet shelter. The unit's Type II enrichment on how to create and analyze games of chance was the perfect preface to this Type III experience. The carnival consists of different types of games. These games need to appear fair so the carnival-goers will want to play, but in reality must be unfair so that rather than always giving away prizes, the students will be collecting money for their charity—an intriguing challenge for students. They decided to host the carnival as a Family Math Event in the evening and eagerly began planning and creating their games using the mathematics they had learned in *What Are Your Chances?*

To learn more about Project M³ curriculum units, see the resource section on pages 150–151.

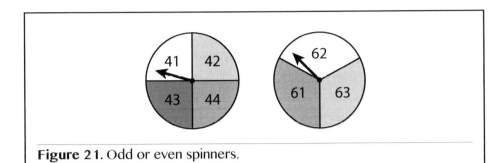

Figure 21. Odd or even spinners.

Middle Grades Type II Enrichment

VIEW FROM THE CLASSROOM

Maria, a seventh-grade math teacher, was tired of hearing her honors class say how boring math was. They were constantly asking, "When are we ever going to have to use this information?" She needed to respond with something better than, "You will need to use it when you study algebra next year." They were just about to start studying laws of exponents and scientific notation, and her prealgebra text gave rules followed by lots of practice examples, exactly what the students were complaining about. She really could not blame them. She needed to find something to excite them and help them see the purpose and beauty of mathematics.

Maria looked for a unit on these topics that would have some practical relevance and spark interest in her students. In the unit *Solve It: Focusing on Equations, Inequalities, and Exponents* (Gavin, Sheffield, & Chapin, 2010), students take on the role of Chief Executive Officer of the Isaac Newton Discovery Center. In this role, they use equations, inequalities, and exponents to solve problems related to their work. They create models, play function games, make business decisions based on costs and profit margins, and set up exhibits (e.g., Life in an Nano-World). She had now caught the attention of her students! She used this unit to create a Type II enrichment experience to explore exponents with her students.

As CEO of the Newton Discovery Center, the first task for the students was to recreate the solar system exhibit that showed the planets orbiting around the sun, including Pluto. Although there was a plaque indicating that Pluto was no longer a planet, they really needed to change the exhibit. They also needed to verify the scientific accuracy of the current model. Were the planets each placed at a correct distance from the sun in the scale model? They were given the following challenge (Gavin et al., 2010): "If you were to create a scale drawing of the solar system with the Earth the size of a dime on a poster for the Center, how big would the sun be? Could you use a wall poster to display the planets and the sun with these dimensions?" (p. 87). They needed to figure this out! They quickly found that using very large numbers to perform calculations was cumbersome. Thus, they saw the need for, and learned about, scientific notation to solve the problem. They were surprised to find that, in this model, the sun would have a diameter of more than 75 inches, and the distance from Uranus to the sun would be almost 2.5 miles! No, a poster would not work. So investigating further, they found most models of the solar system were not drawn to scale due to size limitations.

Their next challenge was to create a display called "Cracking Down on Crime in the Life in a Nano-World." They needed to learn how to work with very small numbers, using scientific notation and negative exponents, to create secret codes to put on dollar bills using quantum dots. These were impossible for forgers to duplicate! Throughout the unit, students saw a purpose for what they were learning, experienced how mathematicians worked in the real world, and used critical and creative thinking to solve problems.

Solve It: Focusing on Equations, Inequalities, and Exponents (Gavin et al., 2010) is part of *Math Innovations*, a middle-grades math program with a focus on critical and creative thinking using the teaching strategies outlined in Chapter 4. To learn more, see the resources section on page 152.

High School Type II Enrichment

VIEW FROM THE CLASSROOM

Alan, a high school enrichment teacher, was working with three math students who wanted to move beyond the topics learned in their honors and AP classes. They were fascinated by what are commonly called "tavern puzzles," disentanglement puzzles historically made by blacksmiths for tavern entertainment. They wondered how they are created and how you can figure out solutions mathematically, if at all possible. Alan wanted to build upon their interest, so he introduced them to the study of *topology*. Eventually they moved from learning about this topic as a Type II enrichment investigation to a Type III project—actually creating their own tavern puzzles and researching marketing options.

One good resource to create Type II experiences for high school students is *The Heart of Mathematics: An Invitation to Effective Thinking* (2005) by Edward Burger and Michael Starbird. This text introduces students to several interesting mathematical topics while inspiring students to actively engage in mathematical thinking. Alan used the chapter titled "Contortions of Space" to encourage his students to learn about topology, to solve interesting puzzles including tavern-type puzzles, and to help them create puzzles of their own.

In summarizing the way all high school education for gifted students should be organized, Dixon, Gallagher, and Olszewski-Kubilius (2009) stated that curriculum and programming needs to be designed to "build motivation through engagement" (p. 182). With respect to secondary mathematics, Sriraman and Steinthorsdottir (2008) indicated that this curriculum is the gateway for an exposure to both breadth and depth of math topics, yet most secondary curricula are still taught in a traditional way devoid of a modeling-based approach used in the real world. Topics such as spherical geometry, topology, graph theory, combinatorics, and statistical modeling can spark the interest of talented students and open up interesting new avenues to explore.

Type IIs as Prologues for Type III Enrichment

No matter what the grade level of your students, Type II Enrichment gives students the opportunity to develop a variety of behaviors similar to those of a practicing professional in a given field of study, in this case mathematics. Not only do they learn the skills and processes that mathematicians use, they also use them to think deeply about mathematical concepts, gain new mathematical knowledge and explore challenging and intriguing mathematical problems. Practicing and refining these skills will assist students as they engage in producing high-quality, innovative Type III projects that we discuss in the next chapter.

CHAPTER 6

Type III Enrichment—
The Capstone of the
Enrichment Triad Model

> When people cannot see the need for what's being taught, they
> ignore it, reject it, or fail to assimilate it in any meaningful way.
> Conversely, when they have a need, then, if the resources for
> learning are available, people learn effectively and quickly.
> —John Seely Brown and Paul Duguid,
> *The Social Life of Information*, 2000

Type III enrichment is the ultimate goal of the Schoolwide Enrichment Model. It is a celebration of student creative productivity. It is what the Three Es are all about. Students start with enjoyment, perhaps even a fascination with a specific area or topic in mathematics. This leads to delving into the topic and learning and using the processes and tools that mathematicians use in this field. In doing so, students become enthusiastic about what they are learning, eager to learn more, eager to create something of value to share with others, and thus enamored with learning itself. What better way to educate our students than give them the incentive to fall in love with a discipline and continue with lifelong learning?

These Type III investigations are different than the typical math project that can be found in textbook ancillary material. Instead they focus on the finding and solving of a real problem that is meaningful to the student and to a broader audience. In the first chapter of this book, we describe the four characteristics that define a Type III investigation, and they are worth repeating here as we explore Type III enrichment in mathematics. These requirements are:

›   personalization of interest,
›   use of authentic methodology,
›   no existing solution or "right" answer, and
›   designed to have an impact on an audience other than, or in addition to, the teacher.

In this type of inquiry project, students take the lead. They act as the first-hand inquirer and think, act, and feel as mathematicians do. They also work on something of their choosing that has real significance—that has an impact on an audience beyond the teacher. Depending on the project, the audience varies. It can include other members of their school community, such as students, teachers, administrators, and/or school board members; parents; members of the community working in local or state government; members of the business community involved in financial services, engineering, medical, and/or technology fields; and/or members of the broader educational community working in museums, nature centers, or institutions of higher learning. How exciting it is to see a project you have researched and developed come to fruition and be appreciated and often put to use within your community. And research has shown it is this intrinsic (versus extrinsic) motivation and reward that makes a lasting impact on the student (Ryan & Deci, 2000).

Role of the Teacher

Your role in Type III enrichment is very much as a guide, a cheerleader, and a mentor. Sometimes as a guide, you "lead your students to water," introducing them to a new topic in mathematics, like Derek did by providing an opportunity for his students to study probability and like Alan did when introducing his students to topology (see Chapter 5). They provided the Type II activities to help students learn about the topic and use the processes and skills that mathematicians use in this particular field. But the Type III investigation also needs to pique student interest, promote self-regulated engagement, and spark enthusiasm. It is best if the idea itself comes from the students. You often have to work with them to help them determine their special interest and select an area to investigate, then define a problem to investigate and/or narrow down their project to something that is manageable. But in this process you need to remember that you are always the guide, not the leader.

Being a cheerleader for your students is essential. This is a big endeavor for students, especially if it is their first Type III project. You will need to be there for them, applauding their efforts, and encouraging their research and development of the project. Most of all, encourage them to persist when they feel overwhelmed. Persistence is starting to become a lost art with Google at our fingertips and Siri or Alexa instantly available to heed our voice commands. Students need to learn that persistence pays off, and they need your cheerleading to encourage it.

Finally, you serve as a mentor. You need to give feedback to students all along the way. Let them know if they are on the right track. Encourage them to go deeper; raise the bar for them. We all know that students live up to our expectations. Keep your expectations high. Help them "think big" to move beyond a project that has limited scope and applicability to a true Type III investigation. Also provide assistance when barriers arise. They may need help locating resources, finding appropriate experts to answer questions for them, and/or managing their time wisely. You may need to do some research yourself to help them find the experts and expertise they need. You also might be the one to work with other staff so the students are given extra time to work on their project. Type III investigations are very involved, and students get discouraged if they can't find the time due to a full school and afterschool schedule. Advocating for extra time for them could make or break their willingness to continue.

Levels of Type III Enrichment

As Renzulli and Reis (2014) pointed out from their field-tests, the intensity and breadth of a Type III investigation can be different depending upon a student's age and experience with this type of enrichment. For example, Desiree, a second grader, wanted to create a number game to illustrate strategies for mental math solutions to computation problems. Brainstorming with her teacher, she listed all of the things she needed to do: figure out what type of game to create, (board game, card game, dice game, etc.), research different categories, and create problems with answers. Once she had this accomplished, she needed to actually design the game. Next, she field-tested the game with students and then used the results to make revisions. Finally, she invited students in her enrichment class as well as parents to come to a game session and play the game.

At a different level, Toby, a sixth grader, decided to create an app called Math Happens! with fun games to solve interesting math logic problems. He had learned about computer coding in a Type I enrichment activity his teacher had encouraged students to explore, called Hour of Code. He contacted software experts to learn how to write specific programs for his game, then designed and created the game. He planned to field-test the game with a broad audience of students and adults, revise as needed, and finally market it to Apple, backed with the data collected from the research. Both of these examples are real problems for the students, both are quite challenging for each at his or her specific talent development stage, and both involve using the processes and skills of mathematicians as they create and solve challenging problems.

We have also found that students produce higher quality, more creative, and more useful products as they continue to do Type III investigations. Sometimes you will need to help students scale back their ideas on the first project so they can be successful and enjoy the process, knowing the next one will be more involved.

Identifying Student Interests

Teachers can be great talent scouts for students who would benefit from and enjoy doing a Type III investigation. Providing one of the many Type I experiences we outlined in Chapter 3 is a great starting point. You can observe students in action as they participate in a mini-math investigation. You can see the enthusiasm a student has when interacting with a visiting professional, such as an architect or a stockbroker. You can witness the excitement a group of students shows on a field trip to the Museum of Mathematics. And students themselves may come to you and say, "I just loved that experience. I want to be an actuary (or math professor, architect, engineer, computer scientist, etc.) when I grow up. How can I learn more?" These are all telltale signs of readiness for a Type III experience.

Another aid to help determine a student's interest in a specific math topic is a math survey. The SEM-Mathematics Interest Survey on page 76 can provide a starting point for a student conference, which is the next step in planning a Type III investigation. The SEM-Mathematics Instructional Styles Survey along with the SEM-Mathematics Expression Styles Survey will also be helpful for you and your student in planning the type of product and audience that would best suit the student.

Focusing on a Problem/Project— Student Conference

A key variable in determining a problem or project for a Type III investigation is examining multiple possibilities. Conferencing with the student helps you learn more about what each student is really interested in and what piques his or her curiosity, and together you can brainstorm many possible ideas. Some students will come in with lots of ideas or even just one specific project they really want to pursue. Others may need more guidance. The following are some open-ended questions that can be helpful to jumpstart the discussion:

› Tell me about yourself. What do you like to do in your free time?
› What would you like to be when you grow up? Why?
› If you were grown up and using mathematics every day in your job, what math would you like to do?
› What do you like learning about in math?
› What don't you like learning about in math?
› What do you wonder about in math?
› If you could meet a famous mathematician from the past or the present, whom would you choose? What would you like to ask him or her?

Brainstorming many ideas and possibilities during the conference and in follow-up meetings often results in more innovative and meaningful projects.

Another factor to consider is whether the project is doable. If it is too big or too unmanageable for the student, the student can become frustrated and so overwhelmed that he or she gives up. This is the last thing you want to happen. This is an important role for you to play as you guide him or her in the problem/project he or she selects and help him or her create a manageable plan. It is a delicate balance—you definitely want to raise the bar, but you don't want to go so high that the student gives up. At the same time, you want to make sure that the Type III endeavor is a creative process, resulting in an innovative product and/or solution. Although it is certainly possible to learn new math and have fun solving problems in enrichment workbooks, students need to go beyond what they can learn and report from websites and reference books. Their Type III investigation should make a creative contribution that will be of interest and useful to an intended audience.

Use of Authentic Methodology

Once the student has zeroed in on the interest area and specific problem/project to explore in a Type III, the student needs to figure out, "What do I do with this problem/idea for a project?" Some sage advice for students who may seem overwhelmed and do not know where to begin comes from a children's book titled just that, *What Do You Do With a Problem?* (Yamada, 2016):

> When I got face-to face with [the problem], I discovered something. My problem wasn't what I thought it was. I discovered it had something beautiful inside. My problem held an opportunity! It was an opportunity for me to learn and to grow. To be brave. To do something.

Once viewed as an opportunity, students can approach the problem/project in a new light. Remember, the goal is to have them use the authentic methods of the professionals in the field. Good guiding questions to ask your students are: *How would mathematicians approach this problem/project? What have you learned about the way mathematicians think that you can apply here?*

Let's take a look at what mathematicians do with a problem in general. First of all, they view it as an opportunity, and an exciting one at that. How do they work using the processes and skills that we outlined in Chapter 4? It is never an easy road, as some might think. Mathematicians work hard and use their skills to figure it out. They tinker or play around with the problem. They make guesses, try them out, and revise them based on their trials. They wonder about what would happen if they tried to solve the problem a different way. They make models and test them out. They look for patterns and see if they continue. This takes time and can lead to many dead ends. But then, they persist. And often the "aha" moment comes after much trial and error. But when it comes, and it will come to your students as well, it is the best feeling in the world. This is the true joy in studying mathematics.

When mathematicians are working, they are persevering in getting to the solution; they are reasoning and justifying their reasoning, using what they have found while working on the problem. In other words, they are using the processes and skills that are part of a mathematician's repertoire. This is a creative process, flexible and fluid, in which mathematicians relate the problem to what they already know and then figure out what they don't know. They consult with each other about their problem or project, giving each other ideas and asking clarifying questions. They create new questions and find new solutions. They are constantly questioning, experimenting, and evaluating. They think "outside the box." Figure 22, developed by Dr. Linda Jensen Sheffield (Jensen, 1980), illustrates this flexible method of problem solving, which we encourage you to share with your students and help them use to explore a Type III problem.

Role of the Audience

Knowing there is a real purpose for the Type III enrichment students are doing is important. The audience with which students share their final project helps define and shape the investigation itself. Sometimes the audience is actually defined by the project, such as entering a competition. In this case, the challenge is usually given, how you will showcase your solution/invention is detailed, and the judges (the audience) are revealed. Sometimes students know they want to create something specific, such as a math exhibit for a school fair or, more ambitiously, for a local discovery center. But often it is not that easy. If students are struggling to come up with a problem or idea, it can help to ask what kinds of problems or ideas of interest lend themselves to a product they can create and share with an audience that can use it.

For example, a third-grade student may be concerned about the amount of food that is being thrown away in the cafeteria trash. What can she do about this? How can she gather and collect data to show there is a problem and then create a solution? Who would be interested in this? Most importantly, who would be interested that can actually make a change happen? Figuring out that the cafeteria staff, administration, and school board would find this information useful and be willing and able to make improvements based on the data and suggestions gives focus to the project. We encourage you to spend time discussing the audience with your student. The audience helps direct the questions to investigate and the shape the product will take.

A Type III investigation is no ordinary problem or project. The fact that the student is working on something that will benefit a specific audience is exciting and makes it all the more worthwhile. You will be amazed at how motivating this is for your students—a great deal of work, yes, but done with engagement, enthusiasm, and providing enjoyment to all involved.

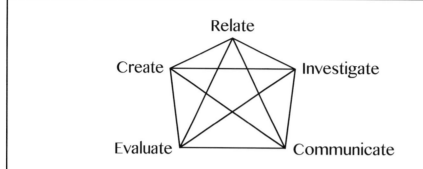

Heuristic for Innovative and Creative Mathematics (Jensen, 1980).

Figure 22. Heuristic for innovative and creative mathematicians. From *A Five-Point Program for Gifted Education*, by L. R. Jensen, 1980, paper presented at the International Congress on Mathematical Education, Berkeley, CA. Copyright 1980 by L. R. Jensen Sheffield. Reprinted with permission.

Making a Plan

A management plan will help students organize the process and focus on the steps needed to create their final product. It is essentially a written contract between you and your students that solidifies their commitment to the project and keeps them on track. They should communicate what the problem is and how they are going to address it with the investigation they conduct and the product/solution they create. They should discuss the audience, who it is, how they will share the results/product, and how they see this benefitting the audience. They should identify resources, persons, places, websites, books, etc., that will be helpful. They will undoubtedly add to these as the project advances. We suggest using the Type III Math Management Planner in Handout 4 at the end of this chapter.

As a guide and mentor, your role is invaluable in helping students make the plan. You can also provide assistance in finding appropriate resources, help them get access to these resources, and make effective use of them. In fact, identifying and making effective use of resources is key to the success of the project. You should also build in regular conference dates to check in on progress, with the understanding that the student can always come to you for advice at any time.

Completing the Project

We remind you to be the guide on the side, the cheerleader, and the mentor. The bigger the problem/project, the more involved the student needs to become, and the more time needed to devote to the project. Dead ends can lead to discouragement. No right answer or no solution in sight can also be unsettling and confusing. Remind students that this is what real problems do and this is what mathematicians also face. Encourage them to keep going, lend a hand when you can, point them in the direction of appropriate resources, including people, places, websites, and books to help them. The sense of accomplishment students gain from completing a Type III investigation—seeing their final product, the reaction of their audience, and its broader impact—is evidence of teaching and learning at their best.

Examples of Type III Math Enrichment Across the Grades

Type III enrichment investigation can use mathematics in different ways. Some Type III investigations involve only mathematics, for example, setting up a new math exhibit exploring really big numbers for a local discovery center. However, many use mathematics to solve problems in a variety of different fields, just as Amber in Chapter 1 used equations to further understand black holes and Chris wrote a software program to aid in determining the growth of a cancer cell. We have mentioned a few Type III math enrichment projects throughout the book. To give you an idea of the flexibility, variety, and creative productivity of Type IIIs in mathematics, we share a few more with views from the classroom. In addition we provide a list of competitions and other resources on page 156.

VIEW FROM THE CLASSROOM—GRADE 3

Erik wanted to get students in his third-grade math enrichment class involved in a Type III investigation. The closest his students came to doing independent projects was writing book reports and researching information about their favorite animal and creating a poster. This was going to be a challenge for them, and he knew they would be excited about it but also would need some guidance.

They had been learning about estimation and measurement in their math class, so he decided to introduce them to Fermi problems. Fermi problems, named after the Italian physicist Enrico Fermi, are problems in which there is not an exact solution, but they can be answered using estimation, number sense, and investigation. Because these problems are without an exact answer and require a good deal of planning and high-level mathematical thinking to come up with an answer, Erik thought a Fermi problem would be a great way to introduce Type IIIs. In addition, these enrichment students loved big numbers and were always asking him about them. How big is a zillion? What is a googol? Is there a biggest number? Is there a smallest number? What is infinity? So a Fermi Problem, which usually involves large quantities, would surely interest them.

After explaining what a Fermi problem was, he gave them two examples:

› How many water balloons does it take to fill our classroom?
› How many turkeys are eaten on Thanksgiving Day in the United States?

Next, Erik asked his students what Fermi problem they would like to work on as a group. After much discussion, they chose one that also had meaning for them. Hurricane Harvey had landed in Houston and devastated the area. They wanted to send some care packages to families: *How many care packages could be shipped in a semi-trailer truck to people whose homes have just been destroyed by Hurricane Harvey in Houston?*

Depending on how many packages they needed, they would enlist their school and extend to the community to gather the materials. Erik had a friend who owned a semi-trailer truck and was willing to fill two-thirds of his truck with the materials. He traveled to Houston once a month. This made the problem even more interesting! It certainly had all of the criteria of a Type III investigation: personal interest, a need to use the methods mathematicians use to figure out the answer, no exact answer, and an audience that would definitely benefit from their final product.

They brainstormed questions they needed to answer:

› What should they put in the care packages that victims most needed and would be available and easy for donors to gather?
› How big will the truck be? What should they be measuring? Height? Length? Width? Capacity? Weight?

> › How can they figure out how many packages would fit? What would be the best shape for the package? Should they measure the height of the package? Length? Width? Weight?

They were off and running. They planned to present their findings to the school faculty and administration as a start and then create posters to encourage everyone to contribute. Parents got involved, and town supermarkets and local pharmacies donated. Even town officials and the police and fire departments donated. It really had the whole community coming together.

Students used the problem-solving skills mathematicians employ, not only to figure out the mathematics involved but also to solve the logistics of finding donors and gathering the materials. A management plan was very helpful in working through all the stages of the project It helped them stay focused and meet their deadlines, which were tight in order to provide the help to Houston families in a timely manner. See their Management Planner in Figure 23. They were excited to see their estimate come very close to the actual amount needed. They also learned a lesson in how generous people can be, especially the truck driver!

VIEW FROM THE CLASSROOM—GRADE 6

Skyler and Stephanie, sixth-grade math students, were fascinated by robotics. They had tinkered around playing computer games with robots, but they wanted more . . . they wanted to be part of a robotics team. They approached their math teacher, Ms. Henchley, and asked if she would consider starting a team. She thought this was the perfect opportunity to create an enrichment cluster during the open block period offered twice a week. She had heard that the FIRST (For Inspiration and Recognition of Science and Technology) non-profit sponsored robotics competitions called FIRST LEGO League challenges (http://firstlegoleague.org). She thought this would be an ideal way to provide enjoyment and challenge to math students interested in using the Type II skills in mathematics they were working on in a Type III experience.

SEM TYPE III MATH MANAGEMENT PLANNER

PURPOSE

Describe the problem you want to solve/the idea you want to investigate.

How many care packages could be shipped in a semi-trailer truck to people whose homes have just been destroyed by Hurricane Harvey in Houston?

AUDIENCE

What individuals/groups might be interested in your results/product? How will you contact them? List names and contact information.
  › Truck Driver (our teacher has contact information)
  › Red Cross in Houston to distribute packages (contact through our local Red Cross organization)
  › Teachers, school administrators, parents, and community organizations who might be willing to donate supplies

PRODUCT

What form will your final product take? How will you share this with your intended audience?
  › PowerPoint presentation to teachers and administrators in our school
  › Visits, phone calls, and posters to gather donations
  › Create and fill truck with care packages

GETTING STARTED

What are your first steps? What information do you need to get started?
  › Contact truck driver to find out how big the truck is
  › What dimension(s) of the truck do we need to figure out how many packages we need? Height? Length? Width? Capacity? Weight?
  › How can we figure out how many packages would fit?
  › What would be the best shape for the package?
  › Where can we get the containers we need?

Figure 23. Sample SEM Management Planner.

RESOURCES

List the resources (books, websites, etc.) and the people (names and contact information) you will use that you think will be helpful to provide assistance in your investigation. Add to this list as your investigation progresses.

› Our math textbook and/or online math websites to determine what measures we should be using and how to calculate them (calculators, rulers, and tape measures to help determine measurements)
› Local moving company to determine what size containers are available for shipping
› Local Red Cross to determine what we should be collecting and help determine appropriate packaging arrangement

DATES FOR PROGRESS CONFERENCES

September 5   October 5   October 20

Figure 23. Continued.

The current FIRST LEGO League challenge for this age group was on hydrodynamics. Students would need to build, test, and program a robot using LEGO MINDSTORMS that was capable of solving a series of missions related to human water and the global water crisis. They would be able to enter their robot in a competition with students from all over the world. Skyler and Stephanie were excited and enlisted a few friends to join them in this adventure. The problem in this situation was defined by the challenge presented. They would be given a specific problem, such as the removal of a broken water pipe. Students, however, needed to make a management plan to figure out how to solve the problem (which is certainly not apparent) and how to build the robot to provide the solution. Again, there was no one right answer. The audience in this case was comprised of the judges, who assessed the final projects and gave feedback to the students. Students competed at the regional level and could continue to state and national levels depending on their success. Ms. Henchley served as the mentor as she helped students figure out the questions they needed to answer, the resources they needed to use, and how to find them. She was there to provide support, guide them in the right direction, and cheer them on.

There are many competitions at all educational levels that focus on STEM investigations and require the skills that mathematicians use. We have complied a list of our favorite ones that lend themselves to a Type III experience in the Resources on page 156.

VIEW FROM THE CLASSROOM— HIGH SCHOOL

What better way to get a deeper understanding of financial literacy and the mathematics of banking than opening and running a branch in your high school. This is exactly what five high school students, with the help of two of their teachers, did in Hartselle, AL (Bryan, 2017). These seven people interned for 2 weeks in the summer at a local bank and then opened a bona fide branch of the bank in the back of their school library, which was opened for a short period of time daily. The superintendent of schools was the first to open an account! Creating a similar opportunity with a local bank would be a great Type III enrichment experience. Students interested in a career in banking would experience firsthand the workings of a bank, the mathematics involved in issuing credit, giving loans, determining interest rates, etc. One of the Alabama students wanted to be a commercial banker, and his interest was piqued with this experience. Students need to define the steps and questions they need to consider in opening the branch, locate a local bank that would be interested, make effective use of the resources (interning at the bank was a great example of this), and then create an innovative product (the bank branch) for an interested audience (the entire school community). As Walt Disney said, "If you can dream it, you can do it." It just takes imagination, creativity, and a passion to learn and use mathematics.

To review, every Type III investigation needs to be student-directed, and the problem/idea needs to be one the student or group of students has a genuine interest in. The product that is created needs to have an intended audience, beyond the teacher, who will also be interested. Students need to carry out the investigation and deliver the innovative result to the audience. If you and your students think of a Type III enrichment experience as a unique and creative learning process that results in an innovative product or solution, you will be off to a good start. Type III investigations are truly the epitome of the Three Es. Your students will be engaged, enthusiastic, and truly enjoy the learning experience.

HANDOUT 4
SEM Type III Math Management Planner

Purpose

Describe the problem you want to solve/the idea you want to investigate.

> _____

> _____

> _____

> _____

Audience

What individuals/groups might be interested in your results/product? How will you contact them? List names and contact information.

> _____

> _____

> _____

HANDOUT 4, CONTINUED.

Product

What form will your final product take? How will you share this with your intended audience?

_____

_____

_____

_____

Getting Started

What are your first steps? What information do you need to get started? How can you find it?

_____

_____

_____

_____

Resources

List the resources (books, websites, etc.) and the people (names and contact information) that you think will be helpful to provide assistance in your investigation. Add to this list as your investigation progresses.

_____

_____

_____

_____

Dates for Progress Conferences

CHAPTER 7

Implementing the Enrichment Triad Model in Math—Many Pathways for Learning

Students with exceptional mathematical promise must be engaged in enriching learning opportunities during and outside the school day to allow them to pursue their interests, develop their talent, and maintain their passion for mathematics. (NCTM, 2016, p. 1)

As we mentioned in Chapter 1, we do not believe in dictating a specific structure or a prescriptive method to implement the Enrichment Triad Model in your school or classroom. Just as no student is alike, so too teachers are different in their teaching and learning styles and their interests and backgrounds. We want to encourage you to use your own creativity and flexibility in adapting curriculum practices and nurturing math talent in your students. Our three overriding goals, the Three Es of enjoyment, engagement, and enthusiasm, which we talk about often in this book, should be your guide to implementing SEM-Math.

We also recognize that there are school structures within which you need to work and students need to learn. SEM has been used effectively within a variety of different organizations. We discuss these now to help you envision how you can implement SEM-Math, given your particular environment.

Whole-Class Enrichment

Type I activities are usually used to introduce a topic to the entire class. We listed a variety of ways to do this in Chapter 3, such as mini-investigations, field trips, speakers, and online investigations. We recommend enlisting the aid of the math specialist and enrichment specialist in planning these activities. In a "push-in" model for gifted programming, enrichment specialists sometimes take the lead and organize the Type I experience for the whole class. Another way to infuse the Three Es into your regular math class is to replace the content for a unit from your regular math program with a unit that is designed specifically to raise the bar and provide more challenge while at the same time affording your students creative and enjoyable activities. Think of using these new experiences as talent scouting. You are looking to see who is really motivated by such experiences and has a genuine interest in pursuing a specific topic in math or is ready for a more challenging math program/experience. For example, we have seen the use of Project M^2 units described in Chapter 5 to be very effective in identifying young students with math talent who are then given the opportunity to participate in the gifted program in subsequent years.

Enrichment Clusters

Enrichment clusters are an exciting and unique SEM component appropriate for all students. These clusters serve students who share a common interest across grade levels and ability levels. They can be organized and directed by a teacher or administrator, a gifted/enrichment specialist, a math coordinator, a parent, or a community member who has expertise and interest in a specific math area. The clusters are quintessential Enrichment Triad investigations. Students and cluster leader come together based on a common interest to pursue an investigation that is highly motivating and engaging and engenders enthusiasm. The clusters can be implemented in a variety of ways. Some schools set aside a time block of an hour a week, others use a half-day block a week, and some meet daily. Some middle and high schools already have a block of time set aside for electives or special activities that usually rotates every month or semester. This is the perfect place to host an enrichment cluster. Math enrichment clusters come in many varieties. The robotics enrichment cluster, described in the last chapter, that Ms. Henchley created is a great way to find the time during the school day to work with students on something they love and create a product to enter a local, state, national, or even international competition. Creating a cluster to prepare for competitions works well at all grade levels, whether it be Math Olympiad, MATHCOUNTS, Invention Convention, Statistics Poster Competition, the Stock Market Game, or one of the many other math and math-related competitions available. See the Resources section for websites and a listing of several more. Competitions are often an easy way to begin with enrichment clusters because specific guidelines and rules are already established, which give you a way to structure the cluster.

Of course, the cluster doesn't need to revolve around a competition. You need to determine student interest and match it to either your interest and expertise or the appropriate person or professional who has both. Creating an architectural rendering and three-dimensional scale drawing of an important landmark in town with a local architect can be exciting for future engineers, architects, and graphic designers. Some students love intriguing math problems. You can find many that are free and online or purchase hard copies of the games and then create a math games cluster. This can lead to a Type III enrichment experience of creating math games for children and donating them to the local children's hospital. The type of cluster is virtually unlimited and only depends on the interests and imagination of you, your team, and your students.

VIEW FROM THE CLASSROOM

Clara, an enrichment specialist, wanted to encourage students in her elementary school who showed an interest in math. She wanted students to see how much fun math can be and develop a love for the subject that they would carry with them throughout their schooling. She thought a Math Games cluster might do the trick and opened it up to all students in grades 3 through 5.

Students came together twice a week for an hour each time to play games and explore interesting math problems and puzzles. Clara had reviewed the SEM-Math interest surveys that were given to students to determine what kinds of math they were interested in, and she had a variety of activities ready and waiting. Some were card games dealing with numbers and operations (Krypto and the 24 Game). She had an algebra board game called Equate, where students used numbers, variables, and operations to create equations. For the students who loved manipulating objects in space, she also offered the card game,

Set. Students also had the options of playing some of these games online (e.g., https://www.setgame.com/set/puzzle offers a new Set problem each day).

For the first week, Clara spent time explaining each game, and all students got to play a version of the game. She specifically selected math games that could be differentiated by offering varying levels of difficulty. She also had websites with challenging and intriguing problems that students could work on. She set up stations around the room, and students signed up for specific stations each week. Most of them tried several of the stations, but some were enthralled by one or two particular games and came back to these over and over. In fact there was a small group of fifth graders that just loved playing the 24 Game. Through the website for the game, they found out there was a national competition and wanted to enter it. Thus, another enrichment cluster was born to work with students on organizing and competing. Clara was excited to see her students so engaged and enthusiastic about continuing with their math adventures. Below are websites where you can find out more about each game that Clara used:

> Krypto: https://www.brainpop.com/games/primarykrypto
> Set: https://www.setgame.com/set/puzzle
> 24 Game: https://www.24game.com
> Problems of the Week (according to grade level and topic): http://mathforum.org/pows (The National Council of Teachers of Mathematics now manages this site.)
> Equate: http://www.playequate.com

Creating an enrichment cluster, where students who are interested come together and have fun with math games, puzzles, and problems, is a perfect way to nurture the love of math. We have listed some more websites and books in our resource section to help you get started.

An enrichment cluster is also a great way to get community members (e.g., a banker, an actuary, a statistician) involved in working with you and students. It is also an engaging way to tap the potential and interest of administrators. We have witnessed principals and even superintendents mentor students in an enrichment cluster. They love the chance to work directly with students. For more information on enrichment clusters, we recommend *Enrichment Clusters: A Practical Plan for Real-World, Student-Driven Learning* (Renzulli, Gentry, & Reis, 2014).

Pull-Out Gifted/Enrichment Programs

Some school districts have a gifted/enrichment specialist who works directly with identified students during a specific time block. This is an ideal situation in which the Enrichment Triad Model can be implemented with students. We suggest creating a team that involves teachers, the gifted/enrichment specialist, and the district math coordinator or school math coach to identify and service students who have math talent and/or talent potential. The first step is to select students for the program using a variety of measures outlined in Chapter 2, including the Student Math Profile. Then we recommend administering the SEM-Math surveys found in Chapter 3. Finally, the team should work together to decide on how best to meet the needs of the students during the time block allotted. Student groups can be formed by math interest, specific math ability, and/or grade levels. An important element of the SEM is to make sure you decide with students what math topic/investigation to pursue. Deciding how to pursue that topic may require help from the team in order to make sure that the resources used provide challenge, rigor, and especially student enjoyment that engenders enthusiasm.

Flexible Grouping and Curriculum Compacting

There are also ways to work with small groups or individual students within the regular classroom. Flexible grouping in math allows a grade level or individual teacher to identify students who have mastered or nearly mastered a specific unit or topic of instruction that is going to be taught next, such as multiplication of fractions or adding two-digit numbers. Using the unit postassessment as a preassessment is a quick and easy way to identify these students. We encourage you not to require a perfect score. Students who have mastered 80%–85% of the material can pick up the rest quickly and then move on to explore a different topic or a more in-depth and higher level study of the same topic. Preassessing also gives you confidence that your students know the required material and will be able to achieve (probably exceed) the goals of district and state testing. It will be helpful to list specific math standards (objectives) that the student has mastered based on testing evidence. As we mentioned in earlier chapters, do not let preparation for state and district assessments keep you from providing enrichment opportunities for your students. Because students already know the material you are about to teach, you can do both: prepare for the material covered on high-stakes assessments and provide challenging and enjoyable enrichment opportunities that lead to their creative productivity.

Curriculum compacting is great way to orchestrate flexible grouping and foster appropriate differentiated instruction for your students. This is especially helpful when individual students in the group want to pursue different interests in math. Reis, Renzulli, and Burns (2016) recommended starting small with just two or three students. Start by preassessing your students. You can use the unit assessment. Other assessments can include solutions of challenging problems that show understanding of the concepts and/or standardized test scores on questions for the particular content area. The Compactor (Reis et al., 2016) in Figure 24 is a useful tool to organize the compacting process, document that the student has shown mastery of part or most of the math standard about to be studied, and indicate what the enrichment/acceleration plan will be, including how any objectives in the math standard not mastered will be learned. It is a simple three-step process, as indicated on the Compactor Form in Figure 24: Name It, Prove It, and Change It.

Name It tells what mathematics is being considered—what unit chapter and objectives or standards the students has mastered. *Prove It* is where you document student strengths—how you know the student has mastered this content (e.g., performance results that indicate mastery of specific objectives). *Change It* is what the student will pursue instead of working on the material he/she already knows. In this space, you also indicate how he or she will learn objectives not yet mastered. This is where the Enrichment Triad Model comes into play. You will consult with the student on his or her interests and work together to create a plan to pursue alternative studies in math. This may be a Type I, II, or III experience. You and your student may find the SEM-Math Interest Survey, Learning Styles Survey, and Expression Styles Survey helpful here. For a complete description and a how-to guide for curriculum compacting we recommend *Curriculum Compacting: A Guide to Differentiating Curriculum and Instruction Through Enrichment and Acceleration* by Reis et al. (2016).

Individual Education Program Guide		
The Compactor		
Student Name(s):	Grade:	School:
Participating Teachers:		
Name it.	**Prove it.**	**Change it.**
Curriculum Area	Assessment	Enrichment/Acceleration Plans
Name or insert the subject area, unit or chapter, or learning standards that are the focus for compacting.	List the assessment tools and related data that indicates student strengths or was used for preassessment, the results of the preassessment data, and learning standards that have not yet been mastered. Identify pertinent student interests that emerged from inventories or interviews.	Briefly describe the enrichment or acceleration tasks that will be substituted for the compacted curriculum, and any strategies used to ensure student mastery of learning standards and objectives that have not been met through enrichment and acceleration. Explain which strategies will be used to support, or coach student learning at more advanced levels.

Figure 24. The Compactor. From *Curriculum Compacting: A Guide to Differentiating Curriculum and Instruction Through Enrichment and Acceleration* (2nd ed., p. 34), by S. M. Reis, J. S. Renzulli, and D. E. Burns, 2016, Waco, TX: Prufrock Press. Copyright 2016 by Prufrock Press. Reprinted with permission.

VIEW FROM THE CLASSROOM

Peter, a fifth-grade teacher, had a few students in his class who excelled in math. Devon was one of them. He had a very strong handle on computation with all whole numbers, decimals, and even fractions, and he loved working with numbers. Peter knew he would be bored studying the units in their math program that focused on these topics. Yet, mastery of all of the concepts in these units was essential to do well on the grade 5 district and state assessments. So he decided to preassess Devon and two other students to see if they could compact out of the regular curriculum. Sure enough, they did. Peter also took into account their keen interest in saving the environment when he decided to provide a Type II enrichment experience. Together they would explore a challenging unit, *The Environment Matters: Making Sense of Percents* (Gavin, Sheffield, Chapin, & Dailey, 2015), focused on learning about percentages, an advanced math concept for fifth graders, while learning about and working on recycling and water conservation at both school and home. Devon was excited. Peter used the Compactor in Figure 25 to document mastery of the standards and plan for the enrichment experience.

Cluster Grouping

Some schools use cluster grouping. Cluster grouping is similar to flexible grouping except the students have generally been identified as gifted and talented for their grade level prior to starting the school year and are placed together in one classroom. Ideally, the classroom teacher has training in gifted education and, in this case, also in mathematics. If a group of students has been specifically identified with math talent or math talent potential, the teacher has an easier task in finding appropriate challenging and creative experiences for these students. And we emphasize that the mathematics these students study should be different —more advanced, more in-depth, and more complex — than what the remainder of the class studies. If students have been identified using general IQ or reading scores, for example, then the group can be as diverse as the entire

Individual Education Program Guide

The Compactor

Student Name(s): Devon	Grade: 5	School: Elmwood Elementary

Participating Teachers: Mr. Nichols (grade 5 teacher), Ms. Gillin (Math Coordinator), Mr. DiCicco (Enrichment Specialist)

Name it.	Prove it.	Change it.
Curriculum Area	**Assessment**	**Enrichment/Acceleration Plans**
Name the subject area, unit, chapter, or learning standards that are the focus for compacting.	List the assessment tools and related data that indicate student strengths and interests. List the preassessment data and learning standards that have not yet been mastered.	Briefly describe the strategies used to ensure mastery of the standards that have not yet been mastered. Name the enrichment or acceleration tasks that will be substituted for the compacted curriculum.
Perform operations with multi-digit whole numbers and with decimals to hundredths. 5.NBT.B.5, 5 NBT.B.6 and 5.NBT.B.7	Unit preassessments: Whole numbers—100% Decimals—100% Multiplication of fractions—85%	Standard 5.NF.B.6 will be incorporated into Type II enrichment.
Use equivalent fractions as a strategy to add and subtract fractions. 5.NF.A.1, 5.NF.A.2	Standards not yet mastered 5.NF.B.6: solve real world problems involving multiplication of fractions with visual models and equations.	Devon is eager to join two other advanced students to explore the Project M^3 enrichment unit, *The Environment Matters: Making Sense of Percents.* Students will gain a conceptual understanding of percents including relationships between fractions, decimals and percents and operations with percents. They will use models and equations to solve contextual percent problems.
Apply and extend previous understanding of multiplication to multiplication of fractions. 5.NF.B.3, 5.NF.B.4.A, 5.NF.B.4.B, 5.NF.B.5.A, 5.NF.B.5.B, 5.NF.B.6	SEM-Math surveys indicated Devon really likes working with fractions and decimals and wanted to learn more about percents. He enjoys collaborating with other students and writing and talking about math. Mr. Nichols also knew that he was very interested in protecting the environment and had organized a recycling project for his Boy Scout troop.	While exploring land and water conservation, they will make mathematical models, play percent games, perform experiments, and create energy and water conservation plans to implement in their homes.

Figure 25. Sample completed Compactor form. Adapted from *Curriculum Compacting: A Guide to Differentiating Curriculum and Instruction Through Enrichment and Acceleration* (2nd ed., p. 34), by S. M. Reis, J. S. Renzulli, and D. E. Burns, 2016, Waco, TX: Prufrock Press. Copyright 2016 by Prufrock Press. Adapted with permission.

class in math ability, and curriculum compacting to meet the needs of individual students will work. However, it is often amazing to see how some students who might not have math strengths to begin with are inspired by the motivational activities and enthusiasm of their group partners as they engage in Type I, II, and III experiences. We see time and time again how students rise to the challenge, especially when their interest is piqued and math is all of a sudden fun and connected to their world. Keep in mind what NCTM (2016) put forth in its position statement, *Providing Opportunities for Students with Exceptional Mathematical Promise*:

> Exceptional mathematical promise is not a fixed trait; rather it is fluid, dynamic, and can grow and be developed; it also varies by mathematical topic. Exceptional mathematical promise is evenly distributed across geographic, demographic, and economic boundaries. (p. 1)

Be on the lookout for emerging talent and interest in all of your students.

Gifted Mathematics Classes, Gifted Academies, and Specialized Schools

You may be fortunate enough to be part of a learning community that provides special classes for gifted students. There are different types. Some school settings provide special math classes in lieu of the regular math class, such as some elementary gifted programs focused on math, honors math classes in middle and high school, and advanced placement classes in high schools. Other educational institutions, like the Illinois Mathematics and Science Academy, provide services to students identified as gifted in certain or all STEM disciplines. There are also gifted academies, such as Renzulli Academies, that provide an enriched and accelerated curriculum in all subject areas to students identified as gifted or with gifted potential.

In these environments, we encourage you to expand on the Type I, II, and III experiences we have outlined in prior chapters. At the primary and elementary levels, we have witnessed gifted academies successfully use advanced units from Projects M^2 and M^3 as their core curriculum and supplement with other content to make sure all concepts associated with grade-level standards are achieved. Math teachers in all of these schools should consider themselves math enrichment specialists providing engaging learning environments that will ignite and fuel students' love for mathematics and provide the rigor and challenge that talented students need and on which they thrive. You will need to help your mathematically gifted students move through the math program at a faster pace using curriculum compacting, while at the same time making sure they delve into the mathematics more deeply and work on more complex problems within each topic. This is especially true at the elementary level.

TEACHER TIP!

Moving a student quickly through two or three grade levels in one school year using the basic textbook without adding the challenge of critical and creative thinking deprives the student of the rich mathematics he or she deserves. In this way, students do not understand the way mathematicians approach the study of math. They miss out on the joy of discovery of new mathematics!

Even with adding more depth, most gifted students can progress quickly enough to allow time for the study of new topics using Type II and III enrichment. Mentors, including college students majoring in math (a bonus if they are also studying to be teachers) and/or university math professors, can help provide the high-level mathematics needed as students progress through the grades and begin studying advanced college mathematics.

Cocurricular Programs

If your school is not an SEM school or does not provide opportunity for introducing Type I, II, and III experiences during the school day, do not lose heart. Where there is a will, there is a way! We have seen teachers implement many of the Type I, II, and III experiences as before- or afterschool clubs, Saturday programs, and summer programs. Preparing for competitions, such as Math Olympiads and Invention Convention, is a perfect example. And the extra time and effort that go into organizing these activities pay off in the positive difference they can make in a student's life.

VIEW FROM THE CLASSROOM

Colleen is a fourth-grade classroom teacher who knew she had students that needed to be challenged in math. She worked in a poor, urban school with a large English as a Second Language (ESL) population. She struggled in her daily math class to meet the needs of all of her students. The gifted program that once existed in the district no longer existed due to budget cuts. So she and her fourth-grade teaching colleagues decided to create an afterschool math club and open it to fourth-grade students who were interested in math and also had shown promise of math talent in class and/or on standardized tests, including a nonverbal ability test that measured analytical thinking. She was part of the research field-testing for the Project M³ curriculum units and knew the units motivated her students and provided the advanced mathematics they needed. She worked with a local insurance company to gain the necessary funds for materials. Then she dove in.

Her club, *At the Mall With Algebra*, used the Project M³ unit with the same title (Gavin, Chapin, Dailey, & Sheffield, 2015a) to help her students learn about algebra. Students could not wait to learn "high school math." They learned about the different uses for a variable with engaging card tricks. They learned to write and solve equations, both single equations and sets of equations in a variety of ways, using critical thinking and reasoning ability rather than memorizing steps to follow. Then, to showcase their learning, they created a mall as a culminating project where their families and other school personnel came to shop. They decided on the kinds of shops they would have and designed the spaces. As shop owners, they created posters with equations to advertise prices and discounts for their goods. Families visited the shops and had to solve equations in one and two variables in order to find out the prices for the objects they wanted to buy. What fun! When shopping was completed, students acting like mathematicians presented their posters, how they created the equations, and how they recommended solving them. There was a variety of ways to solve the equations, some more efficient than others. They had learned new high-level mathematics and learned how to write about it and talk about it using appropriate mathematical vocabulary—just as mathematicians would. They were off to a great start, understanding algebra as a way of thinking to extend our number system, as opposed to a list of procedures to memorize. And the best part was that they had a wonderful time doing it.

In summary, there are a variety of programming options that afford the opportunity to implement the Enrichment Triad Model and ensure that students are involved in the Three Es in their mathematics school experiences. You will know you are successful when you see students genuinely enjoying math, engaged in their learning, and enthusiastic to share and continue. We knew we had achieved our goal when one of our Project M³ students told her fellow students, "When I am in M³, I am in heaven." She was in an urban school with limited resources and might otherwise not have had an opportunity to see the beauty of mathematics, to know she was good at it, and to begin a love affair with the subject. So just get started no matter what your school setting is, and we assure you, you will also experience the Three Es along with your students.

A Final Note to Our Readers

ENJOY YOUR JOURNEY!

We hope you have enjoyed this book and have been inspired to try some of the teaching strategies and resources that we described. As you witnessed in the many vignettes in "View From the Classroom," these strategies are able to transform your math classroom into a joyful learning experience for you and your students.

We encourage you to start small, perhaps with one of the Type I experiences we outline in Chapter 3. Then move on to Type II and Type III experiences with your students. Use the SEM-Math Interest, Instructional Styles, and Expression Styles surveys in Chapter 3 to help discover what motivates your students. Talk with your students and plan together some investigations that will encourage them to enjoy math, get engaged, and become enthusiastic about the subject and their math class. Use the resources we have compiled to support you. Give your students the opportunity to enjoy math and to think and act like mathematicians. Encourage them to create new and exciting products for real audiences. It will make a positive difference in how they learn and how they view mathematics.

Always be on the lookout for students with math talent and talent potential. Use the Student Math Profile in Chapter 2 to help you. Find ways to provide challenging and engaging investigations to develop their math talent and fuel their interest into passion. You are searching for our future mathematicians who are vital to making this world a better place in which to live.

A teacher can make a world of difference in a student's life. We hope our book helps you do just that and nurture in your students a love of mathematics that extends beyond math to a lifelong love of learning.

—Kathy and Joe

References

Baum, S., Gable, R., & List, K. (1998). *Chi square, pie charts, and me*. Mansfield Center, CT: Creative Learning Press.

Bloom, B. S., & Sosniak, L. A. (1981). Talent development vs. schooling. *Educational Leadership, 38*, 86–94.

Bochner, A., & Bochner, R. (2007). *The new totally awesome business book for kids*. New York, NY: Morrow.

Bryan, S. (2017). *Hartselle High students operate Redstone Federal Credit Union's first in-school branch*. Retrieved from http://whnt.com/2017/09/05/hartselle-high-students-operate-redstone-federal-credit-unions-first-in-school-branch

Burger, E. B., & Starbird, M. (2005). *The heart of mathematics: An invitation to effective thinking* (2nd ed.). Emeryville, CA: Key College.

Callahan, C. M., Hunsaker, S. L., Adams, C. A., Moore, S. D., & Bland, L. C. (1995). *Instruments used in the identification of gifted and talented students*. Storrs: University of Connecticut, The National Research Center on the Gifted and Talented.

Casa, T. M., Firmender, J. M., Gavin, M. K., & Carroll, S. R. (2017). The influence of challenging geometry and measurement units on the mathematics achievement of kindergarteners. *Gifted Child Quarterly, 61*, 52–72.

Chapin, S. H., O'Connor, C., & Anderson, N. C. (2013). *Talk moves: A teacher's guide for using classroom discussions in math* (3rd ed.). Sausalito, CA: Math Solutions.

Csikszentmihalyi, M. (1990). The domain of creativity. In M. A. Runco & R. S. Albert (Eds.), *Theories of creativity* (pp. 190–212). London, England: Sage.

Csikszentmihalyi, M. (1999). Implications of a systems perspective for the study of creativity. In R. J. Sternberg (Ed.), *Handbook of creativity* (pp. 313–335). New York, NY: Cambridge University Press.

Davidson, J. E., & Sternberg, R. J. (1984). The role of insight in intellectual giftedness. *Gifted Child Quarterly, 28,* 58–64.

Delcourt, M. A. B. (1993). Creative productivity among secondary school students: Combining energy, interest, and imagination. *Gifted Child Quarterly, 37,* 23–31.

Delcourt, M. A. B. (1994). Creative/productive behavior among secondary school students: A longitudinal study of students identified by the Renzulli three-ring conception of giftedness. In R. Subotnik & K. Arnold (Eds.), *Beyond Terman: Longitudinal studies in contemporary gifted education* (pp. 401–436). Norwood, NJ: Ablex.

Delcourt, M. A. B. (2008). Where students get creative-productive ideas for major projects in the natural and social sciences. In B. M. Shore, M. W. Aulls, & M. A. B. Delcourt (Eds.), *Inquiry in education volume II: Overcoming barriers to successful implementation* (pp. 63–92). New York, NY: Routledge.

Dixon, F. A., Gallagher, S. A., & Olszewski-Kubilius, P. (2009). Part III. A visionary statement for the education of gifted students in secondary schools. In F. A. Dixon (Ed.), *Programs and services for gifted secondary students* (pp. 173–184). Waco, TX: Prufrock Press.

Dotterer, A. M., & Lowe, K. (2011). Classroom context, school engagement, and academic achievement in early adolescence. *Journal of Youth and Adolescence, 40,* 1649–1660.

Dunn, R., Dunn, K., & Price, G. E. (1977). Diagnosing learning styles: Avoiding malpractice suits against school systems. *Phi Delta Kappan, 58,* 418–420.

Dweck, C. S. (1986). Motivational processes affecting learning. *American Psychologist, 41,* 1040–1048.

Engel, M., Claessens, A., & Finch, M. A. (2013). Teaching students what they already know? The (mis)alignment between mathematics instructional content and student knowledge in kindergarten. *Educational Evaluation and Policy Analysis, 35,* 157–158.

Field, G. B. (2009). The effects of the use of Renzulli Learning on student achievement in reading comprehension, reading fluency, social studies, and science: An investigation of technology and learning in grades 3-8. *International Journal of Emerging Technologies in Learning, 4*(1), 29–39.

Fletcher, R. (2000). *How writers work: Finding a process that works for you.* New York, NY: HarperCollins.

Fraenkel, J. R., & Wallen, N. E. (2003). *How to design and evaluate research in education* (5th ed.). New York, NY: McGraw-Hill.

Frensch, P., & Sternberg, R. (1992). *Complex problem solving: Principles and mechanisms.* Hillsdale, NJ: Erlbaum.

Gardner, H. (1983). *Frames of mind: The theory of multiple intelligences.* New York, NY: Basic Books.

Gardner, H. (2008). *The mind's new science: A history of the cognitive revolution.* New York, NY: Basic Books.

Gardner, H. (2011). *The unschooled mind: How children think and how schools should teach.* New York, NY: Basic Books.

Gavin, M. K., Casa, T. M., Adelson, J. L., Carroll, S. R., & Sheffield, L. J. (2009). The impact of advanced curriculum on the achievement of mathematically promising elementary students. *Gifted Child Quarterly, 53,* 188–202.

Gavin, M. K., Casa, T. M., Adelson, J. L., & Firmender, J. M. (2013). The impact of advanced geometry and measurement units on the achievement of grade 2 students. *Journal for Research in Mathematics Education, 44,* 478–510.

Gavin, M. K., Casa, T. M., Chapin, S. H., Copley, J. V., & Sheffield, L. J. (2009). *Project M²: Level 1, Unit 1: Exploring shape games: Geometry with Imi and Zani teacher guide.* Storrs: University of Connecticut, Neag Center for Gifted Education and Talent Development.

Gavin, M. K., Casa, T. M., Chapin, S. H., Copley, J. V., & Sheffield, L. J. (2011). *Project M²: Level 1, Unit 1: Exploring shape games: Geometry with Imi and Zani teacher guide.* Dubuque, IA: Kendall Hunt.

Gavin, M. K., Casa, T. M., Firmender, J. M., & Carroll, S. R. (2013). The impact of advanced geometry and measurement units on the mathematics achievement of first-grade students. *Gifted Child Quarterly, 57,* 71–84.

Gavin, M. K., Chapin, S. H., Dailey, J., & Sheffield, L. J. (2015a). *Project M³: At the mall with algebra: Working with variables and equations.* Dubuque, IA: Kendall Hunt.

Gavin, M. K., Chapin, S. H., Dailey, J., & Sheffield, L. J. (2015b). *Project M³: Unraveling the mystery of the MoLi stone: Exploring place value and numeration.* Dubuque, IA: Kendall Hunt.

Gavin, M. K., Chapin, S. H., Sheffield, L. J., & Dailey, J. (2015). *Project M³: What are your chances? Probability in action.* Dubuque, IA: Kendall Hunt.

Gavin, M. K., Dailey, J., Chapin, S. H., & Sheffield, L. J. (2015). *Project M³: Level 4: Getting into shapes student mathematician's journal.* Dubuque, IA: Kendall Hunt.

Gavin, M. K., Sheffield, L. J., & Chapin, S. H. (2010). *Math innovations course 3: Solve it: Focusing on equations, inequalities, and exponents.* Dubuque, IA: Kendall Hunt.

Gavin, M. K., Sheffield, L. J., Chapin, S. H. & Dailey, J. (2015). *The environment matters: Making sense of percents.* Dubuque, IA: Kendall Hunt.

Gentry, M. (2014). *Total school cluster grouping and differentiation: A comprehensive, research-based plan for raising student achievement and improving teacher practices* (2nd ed.). Waco, TX: Prufrock Press.

Getzels, J. W. (1987). Problem finding and creative achievement. *Gifted Students Institute Quarterly, 7*(4), B1–B4.

Glas, E. F. (2002). Klein's model of mathematical creativity. *Science and Education, 11,* 95–104.

Good, C., & Dweck, C. S. (2005). A motivational approach to reasoning, resilience, and responsibility. In R. J. Sternberg & R. F. Subotnik (Eds.), *Optimizing student success in school with the other three Rs: Reasoning, resilience, and responsibility* (pp. 39–56). Charlotte, NC: Information Age.

Greenwood, C. R. (1991). Longitudinal analysis of time, engagement, and achievement in at-risk versus non-risk students. *Exceptional Children, 57,* 521–535.

Gubbins, E. J. (Ed.). (1995). *Research related to the enrichment triad model* (RM 95212). Storrs: University of Connecticut, The National Research Center on the Gifted and Talented.

Hébert, T. P., Sorensen, M. F., & Renzulli, J. S. (1997). *Secondary interest-a-lyzer.* Mansfield Center, CT: Creative Learning Press.

Heiligman, D. (2013). *The boy who loved math: The improbable life of Paul Erdos.* New York, NY: Roaring Brook Press.

Jensen, L. R. (1980, August). *A five-point program for gifted education.* Paper presented at the International Congress on Mathematical Education, Berkeley, CA.

Johnsen, S. K., & Sheffield, L. J. (2013). *Using the Common Core State Standards for Mathematics with gifted and advanced learners.* Waco, TX: Prufrock Press.

Kay, S. (1994). From theory to practice: Promoting problem-finding behavior in children. *Roeper Review, 16,* 195–197.

Kessler, C. (2006). *Hands-on ecology: Real-life activities for kids.* Waco, TX: Prufrock Press.

Kettle, K. E., Renzulli, J. S., & Rizza, M. G. (1998). Exploring student preferences for product development: My Way . . . An Expression Style Instrument. *Gifted Child Quarterly, 42*, 49–60.

Knobel, R., & Shaughnessey, M. (2002). Reflecting on a conversation with Joe Renzulli: About giftedness and gifted education. *Gifted Education International, 16*, 118–126.

Krutetskii, V. A. (1976). *The psychology of mathematical abilities in schoolchildren* (J. Teller, Trans.). Chicago: University of Chicago Press. (Original work published 1968)

LaBanca, F. (2008). *Impact of problem finding on the quality of authentic open inquiry science research projects* (Unpublished doctoral dissertation). Western Connecticut State University, Danbury, CT.

Larkin, J. H., Heller, J. I., & Greeno, J. G. (1980). Instructional implications of research on problem solving. *New Directions in Teaching and Learning, 2*, 51–65.

Levitt, S. D., & Dubner, S. J. (2005). *Freakonomics: A rogue economist explores the hidden side of everything.* New York, NY: Harper.

MacKinnon, D. W. (1964). The creativity of architects. In C. W. Taylor (Ed.), *Widening horizons in creativity* (pp. 359–378). New York, NY: Wiley.

McCurdy, H. G. (1960). The childhood pattern of genius. *Horizon, 2*, 33–38.

Moursund, D., & Sylwester, R. (Eds.) (2013). *Common Core State Standards for K–12 education in America.* Eugene, OR: Information Age Education.

National Center for Education Statistics. (2015). *Highlights from TIMSS and TIMSS Advanced 2015.* Washington, DC: Author.

National Council of Supervisors of Mathematics. (2012). *Improving student achievement in mathematics by expanding opportunities for our most promising students of mathematics* [Position paper]. Aurora, CO: Author.

National Council of Teachers of Mathematics. (1989). *Curriculum and evaluation standards for school mathematics.* Reston, VA: Author.

National Council of Teachers of Mathematics. (2000). *Principles and standards for school mathematics.* Reston, VA: Author.

National Council of Teachers of Mathematics. (2016). *Providing opportunities for students with exceptional mathematical promise* [Position paper]. Reston, VA: Author.

National Governors Association Center for Best Practices, & Council of Chief State School Officers. (2010). *Common Core State Standards for mathematics.* Washington, DC: Author.

National Science Board. (2010). *Preparing the next generation of STEM innovators: Identifying and developing our nation's human capital.* Arlington, VA: Author.

Neisser, U. (1979). The concept of intelligence. In R. J. Sternberg & D. K. Detterman (Eds.), *Human intelligence* (pp. 179–189). Norwood, NJ: Ablex.

Nicholls, J. C. (1972). Creativity in the person who will never produce anything original and useful: The concept of creativity as a normally distributed trait. *American Psychologist, 27,* 717–727.

Olenchak, F. R. (1988). The schoolwide enrichment model in the elementary schools: A study of implementation stages and effects on educational excellence. In J. S. Renzulli (Ed.), *Technical report on research studies relating to the revolving door identification model* (2nd ed., pp. 201–247). Storrs: University of Connecticut, Bureau of Educational Research.

Olenchak, F. R., & Renzulli, J. S. (1989). The effectiveness of the schoolwide enrichment model on selected aspects of elementary school change. *Gifted Child Quarterly, 32,* 44–57.

Organisation for Economic Co-operation and Development. (2016). *PISA 2015 results in focus.* Paris, France: Author.

Pelleschi, A. (2016). *Mathematician and computer scientist Grace Hopper: STEM trailblazer bios.* Minneapolis, MN: Lerner.

Reis, S. M., Eckert, R. D., McCoach, D. B., Jacobs, J. K., & Coyne, M. (2008). Using enrichment reading practices to increase reading, fluency, comprehension, and attitudes. *Journal of Educational Research, 101,* 299–315.

Reis, S. M., & Renzulli, J. S. (1982). A case for the broadened conception of giftedness. *Phi Delta Kappan, 64,* 619–620.

Reis, S. M., & Renzulli, J. S. (2003). Research related to the Schoolwide Enrichment Triad Model. *Gifted Education International, 18,* 15–40.

Reis, S. M., Renzulli, J. S., & Burns, D. E. (2016). *Curriculum compacting: A guide to differentiating curriculum and instruction through enrichment and acceleration* (2nd ed.). Waco, TX: Prufrock Press.

Reis, S. M., Westberg, K. L., Kulikowich, J. M., & Purcell, J. H. (1998). Curriculum compacting and achievement test scores: What does the research say? *Gifted Child Quarterly, 42,* 123–129.

Renzulli, J. S. (1977a). *The enrichment triad model: A guide for developing defensible programs for the gifted and talented.* Mansfield Center, CT: Creative Learning Press.

Renzulli, J. S. (1977b). The total talent portfolio: Looking at the best in every student. *Gifted Education International, 12,* 58–63.

Renzulli, J. S. (1978). What makes giftedness? Re-examining a definition. *Phi Delta Kappan, 60,* 180–184, 261.

Renzulli, J. S. (1986). The three ring conception of giftedness: A developmental model for creative productivity. In R. J. Sternberg & J. E. Davidson (Eds.), *Conceptions of giftedness* (pp. 53–92). New York, NY: Cambridge University Press.

Renzulli, J. S. (Ed.). (1988). *Technical report of research studies related to the enrichment triad/revolving door model* (3rd ed.). Storrs: University of Connecticut, Teaching the Talented Program.

Renzulli, J. S. (1994). *Schools for talent development: A practical plan for total school improvement.* Mansfield Center, CT: Creative Learning Press.

Renzulli, J. S. (1997). *Interest-a-Lyzer family of instruments.* Waco, TX: Prufrock Press.

Renzulli, J. S. (2005). The three-ring conception of giftedness. In R. J. Sternberg & J. E. Davidson (Eds.), *Conceptions of giftedness* (2nd ed., pp. 246–279). New York, NY: Cambridge University Press.

Renzulli, J. S. (2010). Unterrichtsfreiheit [Freedom To Teach]. *Swiss Gifted Journal, 3*(1), 5–13.

Renzulli, J. S. (2012). The Multiple Menu Model: A guide for developing differentiated curriculum. In C. M. Callahan, & H. Hertberg-Davis (Eds.), *Fundamentals of gifted education: Considering multiple perspectives* (pp. 263–276). New York, NY: Routledge.

Renzulli, J. S., & Dai, D. Y. (2001). Abilities, interests, and styles as aptitudes for learning: A person-situation interaction perspective. In R.J. Sternberg & L. Zhang (Eds.), *Perspectives on thinking, learning, and cognitive styles* (pp. 23–46). London, England: Earlbaum.

Renzulli, J. S., & Delisle, J. R. (1982). The revolving door model of identification and programming for the academically gifted: Correlates of creative production. *Gifted Child Quarterly, 25,* 89–95.

Renzulli, J. S., Foreman, J. L., & Brandon, L. E. (2017). *Things my child likes to do.* Waco, TX: Prufrock Press.

Renzulli, J. S., Gentry, M., & Reis, S. M. (2014). *Enrichment clusters: A practical plan for real-world, student-driven learning* (2nd ed.). Waco, TX: Prufrock Press.

Renzulli, J. S., Hartman, R. K., & Callahan, C. M. (1971). Teacher identification of superior students. *Exceptional Children, 38,* 211–214.

Renzulli, J. S., Heilbronner, N. N., & Siegle, D. (2010). *Think data: Getting kids involved in hands-on investigations with data-gathering instruments.* Waco, TX: Prufrock Press.

Renzulli, J. S., & Reis, S. M. (1985). *The schoolwide enrichment model: A comprehensive plan for educational excellence.* Mansfield Center, CT: Creative Learning Press.

Renzulli, J. S., & Reis, S. M. (1994). Research related to the schoolwide enrichment model. *Gifted Child Quarterly, 38,* 2–14.

Renzulli, J. S., & Reis, S. M. (1997). *The schoolwide enrichment model: A how-to guide for educational excellence* (2nd ed.). Mansfield Center, CT: Creative Learning Press.

Renzulli, J. S., & Reis, S. M. (2014). *The schoolwide enrichment model: A how-to guide for talent development* (3rd ed.). Waco, TX: Prufrock Press.

Renzulli, S.J., Siegle, D., Reis, M. S., Gavin, M. K., & Sytsma Reed, R. E. (2009). An investigation of the reliability and factor structure of four new scales for rating the behavioral characteristics of superior students. *Journal of Advanced Academics, 21,* 84–108.

Renzulli, J. S., Smith, L. H., White, A. J., Callahan, C. M., & Hartman, R. K. (1976). *Scales for rating the behavioral characteristics of superior students.* Mansfield Center, CT: Creative Learning Press.

Renzulli, J. S., Smith, L. S., White, A. J., Callahan, C. M., Hartman, R. K., Westberg, K. L., Gavin, M. K., Reis, S. M., Siegle, D. & Sytsma Reed, R. E. (2013). *Scales for rating the behavioral characteristics of superior students* (3rd ed.). Waco, TX: Prufrock Press.

Renzulli, J. S., & Sullivan, E. E. (2009). Learning styles applied: Harnessing students' instructional style preferences. In L. Zhang & R. J. Sternberg (Eds.), *Perspectives on the nature of intellectual styles* (pp. 209–232). New York, NY: Springer.

Reyes, M. R., Brackett, M. A., Rivers, S. E., White, M., & Salovey, P. (2012). Classroom emotional climate, student engagement, and academic achievement. *Journal of Educational Psychology, 104,* 700–710.

Ryan, R. M., & Deci, E. L. (2000). Self-determination theory and the facilitation of intrinsic motivation, social development, and well-being. *American Psychologist, 55,* 68–78.

Saunders, W. M., & Goldenberg, C. (2010). Research to guide English Language Development instruction In D. Dolson & L. Burnham-Massey (Eds.), *Improving education for English learners: Research-based approaches.* Sacramento, CA: California Department of Education Press.

Schoenfeld, A. H., & Herrmann, D. J. (1982). Problem perception and knowledge structure in expert and novice mathematical problem solvers. *Journal of Experimental Psychology, 8*, 484–494.

Sheffield, L. J. (Chair), Bennett, J., Berriozabal, M., DeArmond, M., & Wertheimer, R. (1999). Report of the task force on the mathematically promising. In L. J. Sheffield (Ed.), *Developing mathematically promising students* (pp. 309–316). Reston, VA: The National Council of Teachers of Mathematics.

Shetterly, M. L. (2016). *Hidden figures: The American dream and the untold story of the black women mathematicians that helped win the space race*. New York: NY: Morrow.

Shore, B. M., Delcourt, M. A. B., Syer, C. A., & Schapiro, M. (2008). The phantom of the science fair. In B. M. Shore, M. W. Aulls, & M. A. B. Delcourt (Eds.), *Inquiry in education: Overcoming barriers to successful implementation* (Vol. II, pp. 93–118). New York, NY: Routledge.

Sowell, E. J., Bergwell, L., Zeigler, A. J., & Cartwright, R. M. (1990). Identification and description of mathematically gifted students: A review of empirical research. *Gifted Child Quarterly, 34*, 147–154.

Sriraman, B. (2002). How do mathematically gifted students abstract and generalize mathematical concepts? *NAGC 2002 Research Briefs, 16*, 83–87.

Sriraman, B. (2003). Mathematical giftedness, problem solving, and the ability to formulate generalizations: The problem-solving experiences of four gifted students. *Journal of Secondary Gifted Education, 14*, 151–165.

Sriraman, B. (2004). Discovering a mathematical principle: The case of Matt. *Mathematics in School, 33*(2), 25–31.

Sriraman, B. (2008). Are mathematical giftedness and mathematical creativity synonyms?: A theoretical analysis of constructs. In B. Sriraman (Ed.), *Creativity, giftedness, and talent development in mathematics* (pp. 85–112). Missoula, MT: Information Age.

Sriraman, B., & Steinthorsdottir, O. B. (2008). Mathematics, secondary. In J. A. Plucker & C. M. Callahan (Eds.), *Critical issues and practices in gifted education: What the research says* (pp. 395–407). Waco, TX: Prufrock Press.

Starko, A. J., & Schack, G. D. (1992). *Looking for data in all the right places: A guidebook for conducting original research with young investigators*. Waco, TX: Prufrock Press.

Sternberg, R. J. (1984). Toward a triarchic theory of human intelligence. *Behavioral and Brain Sciences, 7*, 269–287.

Sternberg, R. J. (1988). Three facet model of creativity. In R. J. Sternberg (Ed.), *The nature of creativity* (pp. 125–147). Boston, MA: Cambridge University Press.

Sternberg, R. J. (1990). Thinking styles: Keys to understanding student performance. *Phi Delta Kappan, 71,* 366–371.

Sternberg, R. J., & Davidson, J. E. (Eds.). (1986). *Conceptions of giftedness.* New York, NY: Cambridge University Press.

Sternberg, R. J., & Davidson, J. E. (Eds.). (2005). *Conceptions of giftedness* (2nd ed.). New York, NY: Cambridge University Press.

Stewart, I. (2017). *Significant figures: The lives and work of great mathematicians.* New York, NY: Basic Books.

Thorndike, E. L. (1921). Intelligence and its measurement. *Journal of Educational Psychology, 12,* 124–127.

Tomlinson, C. A. (1995). Deciding to differentiate instruction in middle school: One school's journey. *Gifted Child Quarterly, 39,* 77–78.

Tomlinson, C. A. (2000). Reconcilable differences? Standards based teaching and differentiation. *Educational Leadership, 58*(1), 6–11.

Treffinger, D. J. (1998). From gifted education to programming for talent development. *Phi Delta Kappan, 79,* 752–755.

Wang, M. T., & Holcombe, R. (2010). Adolescents' perceptions of school environment, engagement, and academic achievement in middle school. *American Educational Research Journal, 47,* 633–662.

Westberg, K. L. (1991). *The effects of instruction in the inventing process on students' development of inventions.* Unpublished doctoral dissertation, University of Connecticut, Storrs.

Yamada, K. (2016). *What do you do with a problem?* Seattle, WA: Compendium.

Zimmerman, B. J. (1998). Developing self-fulfilling cycles of academic regulation: An analysis of exemplary instructional models. In D. H. Schunk & B. J. Zimmerman (Eds.), *Self-regulated learning: From teaching to self-reflective practice* (pp. 1–19). New York, NY: Guilford Press.

APPENDIX

Additional Resources

This section includes some of our favorite resources to help you in planning Type I, II, and III enrichment for your students.

Books, Book Chapters, and Research Resources

The Schoolwide Enrichment Model

Gavin, M. K., & Renzulli, J. S. (2018). *Using the schoolwide enrichment model in mathematics: A how-to guide for developing student mathematicians.* Waco, TX: Prufrock Press.

Heilbronner, N. N., & Renzulli, J. S. (2016). *The schoolwide enrichment model in science: A hands-on approach for engaging young scientists.* Waco, TX: Prufrock Press.

Housand, A. M., Housand, B. C., & Renzulli, J. S. (2017). *Using the schoolwide enrichment model with technology.* Waco, TX: Prufrock Press.

Reis, S. M., Fogarty, E., & Eckert, R. D. (2008) *The schoolwide enrichment model reading framework.* Waco, TX: Prufrock Press.

Reis, S. M., Renzulli, J. S., & Burns, D. E. (2016). *Curriculum compacting: A guide to differentiating curriculum and instruction through enrichment and acceleration* (2nd ed.). Waco, TX: Prufrock Press.

Renzulli, J. S., Gentry, M., & Reis, S. M. (2014). *Enrichment clusters: A practical plan for real-world, student-driven learning* (2nd ed.) Waco, TX: Prufrock Press.

Renzulli, J. S., & Reis, S. M. (2014). *The schoolwide enrichment model: A how-to guide for talent development* (3rd ed.). Waco, TX: Prufrock Press.

Gifted and Talented Mathematics Education

Assouline, S., Saul, M., & Sheffield, L. J. (Eds.). (2010). *The peak in the middle: Developing mathematically gifted students in the middle grades.* Reston, VA: National Council of Teachers of Mathematics.

Gavin, M. K. (2011). Identifying and nurturing math talent. In F. Karnes & K. Stephens (Eds.), *The practical strategies series in gifted education* (pp. 1–64). Waco, TX: Prufrock Press.

Gavin, M. K. (2014). Project M³: Mentoring mathematical minds. In C. M. Adams & K. L. Chandler (Eds.), *Effective program models for gifted students from underserved populations* (pp. 15–30). Waco, TX: Prufrock Press.

Gavin, M. K. (2016). Mathematics curriculum for gifted learners. In F. Karnes & K. Stephens (Eds.), *Introduction to curriculum design in gifted education* (pp. 151–174). Waco, TX: Prufrock Press.

Gavin, M. K., & Adelson, J. L. (2014). Mathematics gifted education. In J. Plucker & C. M. Callahan (Eds.), *Critical issues and practices in gifted education: What the research says* (2nd ed., pp. 387–412). Waco, TX: Prufrock Press.

Johnsen, S. K., & Sheffield, L. J. (2013). *Using the Common Core State Standards for mathematics with gifted and advanced learners.* Waco, TX: Prufrock Press.

Sheffield, L. J. (Ed.). (1999). *Developing mathematically promising students.* Reston, VA: National Council of Teachers of Mathematics.

Curriculum Resources

Curriculum Units for Talented Math Students

Project M³: Mentoring Mathematical Minds (http://www.projectm3.org; Gavin, Chapin, Dailey, & Sheffield, 2006–2015), published by Kendall Hunt

Publishing Company, is an NAGC award-winning series of 15 research-based units of accelerated and enriched mathematical content for talented math students at the elementary level, funded by a U.S. Department of Education Javits Grant:

Level 3–4 Units:
› *Unraveling the Mystery of the MoLi Stone: Exploring Place Value and Numeration*
› *Awesome Algebra: Looking for Patterns and Generalizations*
› *Digging for Data: Collecting, Displaying and Analyzing Data*
› *Factors, Multiples, and Leftovers: Linking Multiplication and Division*
› *How Big Is Big? Understanding and Using Large Numbers*
› *In Search of the Yeti: Measuring Up, Down, and All Around*

Level 4–5 Units:
› *At the Mall With Algebra: Working With Variables and Equations*
› *Getting Into Shapes: Exploring Relationships Among 2-D and 3-D Shapes*
› *The Tenth Street Pet Sanctuary: Understanding and Using Decimals*
› *Treasures From the Attic: Exploring Fractions*

Level 5–6 Units:
› *Designer Boxes: Exploring Volume and Surface Area*
› *Fun at the Carnival: Using Proportional Reasoning*
› *Record Makers and Breakers: Analyzing Graphs, Tables and Equations*
› *Our Environment Matters: Making Sense of Percents*
› *What Are Your Chances? Probability in Action*

Project M²: Mentoring Young Mathematicians (http://www.projectm2.org; Gavin, Casa, Chapin, & Sheffield, 2010–2017), published by Kendall Hunt Publishing Company, is an NAGC award-winning series of eight units of research-based advanced curriculum in geometry and measurement for students in Kindergarten through grade 2, funded by a National Science Foundation grant:

Level 2 Units:
› *Designing a Shape Gallery: Geometry With the Meerkats*
› *Using Everyday Measures: Measuring With the Meerkats*

› *Shopping at the Bazaar: Connecting Number and Algebra With the Meerkats*

Level 1 Units:
› *Exploring Shape Games: Geometry With Imi and Zani*
› *Creating the School Measurement Fair: Measuring With Imi and Zani*
› *Exploring Number Games: Making Sense of Numbers With Imi and Zani*

Level Kindergarten Units:
› *Exploring Shapes in Space: Geometry With the Frogonauts*
› *Sizing Up the Lily Pad Space Station: Measuring With the Frogonauts*

Math Innovations (Gavin, Chapin, & Sheffield, 2010–2013) is a complete middle-grades curriculum that is designed to engage students in gaining a richer, deeper, and more proficient understanding of mathematics and is aligned with the Common Core State Standards. The curriculum consists of three levels, each featuring five units that focus on a single concept. It addresses critical mathematics areas and supports student learning with a variety of real-life, problem-solving scenarios that are addressed through activities, games, investigations, and projects. The program is published by Kendall Hunt Publishing Company (https://www.kendallhunt.com). "Think Beyond" questions for talented math students are part of every lesson. In addition, the authors have created special advanced sequences of instruction using *Math Innovations* to prepare advanced students for taking algebra in middle school.

Additional Curriculum Resources

Burger E. B., & Starbird, M. (2001). *The heart of mathematics: An invitation to effective thinking* (4th ed.). Hoboken, NJ: Wiley.

This resource is particularly useful for small-group/individual investigations with talented middle and high school students. It includes a variety of interesting math topics outside of the regular curriculum, such as topology, chaos and fractals, and the study of infinity.

Renzulli Learning. (2017). Retrieved from https://renzullilearning.com

The Renzulli Learning System (RLS) is an interactive online teaching and learning tool that provides personalized learning for students. RLS is based on more than 40 years of research and development conducted at the University of Connecticut and field-tested across the country in all types of schools. Renzulli Learning applies gifted and talented teaching strategies and enrichment resources to total school improvement. It enables educators to easily personalize learning and differentiate instruction by using technology to quickly identify student academic strength areas, interests, learning styles, and preferred modes of expression. Once identified, students and their teachers can access a variety of online personalized enrichment activities.

Sheffield, L. J. (2003). *Extending the challenge in mathematics: Developing mathematical promise in K–8 students.* Thousand Oaks, CA: Corwin Press.

The differentiated problems in this book are designed to challenge students in the areas of number, algebra, geometry and measurement, data analysis, and probability. Strategies for assessment are included.

Selected Websites for Providing Math Enrichment

Hour of Code (https://code.org) offers engaging one-hour tutorials in coding for all grade levels.

The Math Forum (http://mathforum.org) is an excellent online resource with a wealth of problems and puzzles, online mentoring, research, team problem solving, collaborations, and professional development. The website is currently being managed by the National Council of Teachers of Mathematics.

MathPickle (http://mathpickle.com) poses visually compelling puzzles and games for students in K–12. The activities are organized by grade and subject and differentiated to provide talented students both challenge and enjoyment.

NCTM's Illuminations (https://illuminations.nctm.org) offers games, interactive activities, including apps, and brainteasers for students in Pre-K through grade 12.

NCTM's Calculation Nation (http://calculationnation.nctm.org) offers online math games involving number and geometry concepts for elementary and middle school students.

NRICH (http://nrich.maths.org) offers free high-level math enrichment activities for students in grades 1–12.

Selected Math Enrichment Games

24 Game (https://www.24game.com): Students in elementary through high school build their computational fluency, problem solving, numbers sense, and critical thinking from addition to algebra with this challenging online game. You can also purchase physical sets of cards.

Set (https://www.setgame.com/set/puzzle): Students in elementary through high school can play this interesting and challenging card game, which involves making sets of shapes with different attributes. The focus is on critical and creative thinking using patterns. This website offers daily challenge puzzles for students. You can also purchase physical sets of cards.

Krypto (https://www.brainpop.com/games/primarykrypto): Students in elementary and middle school can play this card game that involves facility with all four number operations and their use to create equations. You can also purchase a physical copy. In addition, https://www.brainpop.com has many interesting math games to challenge talented students.

Equate (http://www.playequate.com): In this board game for students ages 8 and up and their families, players create equations crossword style. The challenge increases using division or fraction tiles.

PrimePak (http://www.primepakgame.com): This set of cards offers four mathematical thinking games in which students ages 7 and up form factor sets with prime wild cards used for prime numbers.

Conceptual Bingo (http://www.conceptualmathmedia.com/bingo/default. asp): Eleven versions of bingo-style math games for students in K–12. Six questions on each calling card allow for different learning levels and multiple topic coverage.

Selected Websites for Videos of Mathematicians and Their Work

See pages 71–72 for more information.

The Futures Channel (http://thefutureschannel.com) has excellent short video clips of professionals in a variety of fields using mathematics.

Numberphile (http://www.numberphile.com) is a website created by The Mathematical Sciences Research Institute that has videos of mathematicians talking about their interest in mathematics.

TEDEd: Math in Real Life (http://ed.ted.com/series/math-in-real-life) presents a series of interesting clips on math in real life.

Math Enrichment Museum Offerings

See pages 73–74 for more information.

The Exploratorium in San Francisco (https://www.exploratorium.edu/explore) has a collection of online mathematical experiences for virtual visitors housed in the "explore" section of the website.

The Franklin Institute in Philadelphia (https://www.fi.edu) is dedicated to educating about science and technology and details information about all of the exhibits, including photographs and videos. The institute's mobile app also provides access to a library of virtual reality experiences related to the exhibits, from the deep sea to the flight deck of a space shuttle.

MathAlive! (http://mathalive.com/about-the-exhibit) is a traveling math exhibit originally launched at the Smithsonian Institution. The exhibition brings to life the real math behind what kids love most—video games, sports, fashion, music, robotics, and more.

The National Museum of Mathematics (https://momath.org) in New York City has several interactive exhibits, including a circular ride on a square tricycle! It also features traveling exhibits that go around the country (https://mathmidway.org/mm2go).

The Smithsonian (https://www.si.edu) has a website for students to explore featured collections, stories, videos, and more related to their math interests.

The STEAM Portable Hands-On Museum, sponsored by Mobile Ed Productions, (http://www.mobileedproductions.com) is a traveling exhibit that comes to schools and features hands-on station activities in math, science, engineering, and technology for students in grades K–6. Samples of math exhibits include Build-an-Arch, the Pythagorean Theorem Wheel, and Programmable Robots.

Mathematics Competitions

The following is a list of websites that describe mathematics competitions for talented students in elementary, middle, and high school.

Competition	Grade/Age Levels	Website
American Mathematics Competitions	Grades 6–8	https://www.maa.org/math-competitions
American Statistical Association Poster and Project Competitions	Grades K–3, 4–6, 7–9, and 10–12	http://www.amstat.org/asa/education/ASA-Statistics-Poster-Competition-for-Grades-K-12.aspx; http://www.amstat.org/asa/education/ASA-Statistics-Project-Competition-for-Grades-7-12.aspx
Continental Math League	Grades 6, 7, 8 and 9	https://www.cmleague.com
eCybermission	Grades 2–12	https://www.ecybermission.com
EngineerGirl Contests	Grades 3–12	https://www.engineergirl.org
EV Challenge	Grades 6–8	http://www.evchallengekids.org
ExploraVision	Grades K–3, 4–6, 7–9 and 10–12 leagues	https://www.exploravision.org
FIRST LEGO League Challenges	Ages 9–16	http://firstlegoleague.org
Future City Competition	Grades 7–8	http://futurecity.org
INTEL International Science and Engineering Fair	Grades 9–12	https://student.societyforscience.org/intel-corporation
International Mathematical Olympiad	Grades 9–12	https://www.imo-official.org

Competition	Grade/Age Levels	Website
Invention Convention	Grades K–12	http://www.inventionleague.org
Mandelbrot Competition	Grades 9–12	http://www.mandelbrot.org
MATE ROV Underwater Robotics Competition	Grades K–12	https://www.marinetech.org/rov-competition-2
MATHCOUNTS	Grades 6–8	https://www.mathcounts.org/programs/competition-series
Math League	Grades 4–5 and 6–8	http://www.mathleague.com
Math Olympiads	Grades 4–6 and 7–8	http://www.moems.org
National Mathematics Pentathlon Academic Tournaments	Grades K–7	http://www.mathpentath.org
Northeast Science Bowl	Grades 6–8	http://sciencebowl.uconn.edu/m_event.php
Odyssey of the Mind	Grades K–12	http://www.odysseyofthemind.com
Siemens Competition in Math, Science and Technology	Grades 9–12	http://www.siemens-foundation.org/programs/the-siemens-competition-in-math-science-technology

National Programs/Institutes/ Universities That Promote Development of Mathematical Talent

Boston University PROMYS Program
http://www.promys.org

PROMYS is a challenging 6-week summer program designed to encourage ambitious high school students to explore the creative world of mathematics with mentors, including research mathematicians. Returning students also have the opportunity to engage in original research under the mentorship of professional mathematicians.

Davidson Institute
http://davidsongifted.org (search "mathematics")

This website has extensive listings of organizations, competitions, games, problem-solving websites, printed materials, summer and online programs, and other links to develop mathematical talent for creative and promising mathematics students.

Duke University Talent Identification Program (TIP)
http://www.tip.duke.edu

The TIP program conducts talent searches for gifted students in grades 4–6, 7, and 8–10. The program offerings for students in grades 4–12 include a variety of summer courses, scholar weekends, independent study courses, field studies, and online courses, including mathematics.

EngineerGirl
https://www.engineergirl.org

The EngineerGirl website is sponsored by the National Academy of Engineering and is designed to bring national attention to the many opportunities that engineering represents for girls and women. Students can learn about the varied work engineers do, read interviews with women engineers, ask an engineer a question, enter contests and competitions, and learn about scholarships.

Expanding Your Horizons in Science and Mathematics
https://www.eyhn.com

This program hosts, organizes, and offers career-day conferences to nurture girls' interest in science and math courses to encourage them to consider careers in science, technology, engineering, and math. It is designed for girls in grades 5–8.

Johns Hopkins University Center for Talented Youth
http://cty.jhu.edu

The Center for Talented Youth conducts talent searches, offers residential and day programs for students in grades 2–12 at various sites across the country, provides challenging online courses for students in grades K–12, and offers family programs and counseling.

National Association of Math Circles
http://www.mathcircles.org

The Mathematical Sciences Research Institute created the National Association of Math Circles to nurture the growth of Math Circles (informal math programs focused on problem solving and interactive exploration for K–12 students and their teachers, led by mathematicians and other math professionals in the United States). The association provides a list of Math Circles, shares resources to help start and build effective programs, and documents the impact of Math Circles across the nation.

National Consortium of Secondary STEM Schools (NCSSS)
http://www.ncsss.org

The mission of the National Consortium of Secondary STEM schools is to advance STEM education by providing professional development and networking opportunities for educators and learning experiences for students; to serve as a national resource for STEM schools and programs in partnership with educational, corporate, and international organizations; and to inform policymakers on STEM education. There are resources for summer and online programs for gifted students offered by these schools on the website.

Northwestern University Center for Talent Development
http://www.ctd.northwestern.edu

The Center for Talent Development conducts talent searches and has a range of programs for gifted students, including summer programs, Saturday enrichment programs, and online accelerated courses, such as AP and honors mathematics courses. Professional development in gifted education is also available for teachers.

Texas State University Mathworks Honors Summer Math Camp
http://www.txstate.edu/mathworks/camps/Summer-Math-Camps-Infor
    mation/hsmc.html

This program is an intensive multi-summer program for high school students. Students who are returning after their first year have the opportunity to conduct original math research projects in a team that can be submitted to various contests, including the prestigious Siemens Competition in Math, Science, and Technology (http://www.siemens-foundation.org/programs/the-siemens-competition-in-math-science-technology).

University of Connecticut, Renzulli Center for Creativity, Gifted Education and Talent Development

http://www.gifted.uconn.edu/projectm3 or www.projectm3.org

Information on Project M³ curriculum units is available at this website, as well as tips, resources, and links to problem-solving websites for students, parents, and teachers.

http://www.gifted.uconn.edu/projectm2 or www.projectm2.org

Information on Project M² curriculum units is available at this website, as well as tips, resources, and links to problem-solving websites for students, parents and teachers.

University of Iowa Belin-Blank Center

http://www.education.uiowa.edu/belinblank

The Belin-Blank Center conducts a talent search and offers summer programs and weekend programs for high-ability students in grades 2–12. It also has an online AP academy, including AP mathematics courses, and an early entrance to college academy.

Vanderbilt University Programs for Talented Youth

https://pty.vanderbilt.edu

Vanderbilt Programs for Talented Youth offers a variety of advanced summer programs, Saturday sessions, and weekend programs for talented youth in grades K–12, as well as programs for their families and professional development for gifted educators.

National Organizations

The following is a list of national organizations related to mathematics, mathematics education and gifted education.

American Mathematical Society

http://www.ams.org

Association for Women in Mathematics (AWM)

http://sites.google.com/site/awmmath

Davidson Fellows Scholarships
http://www.davidsongifted.org/fellows

Mathematical Association of America
https://www.maa.org

National Association for Gifted Children
http://www.nagc.org

National Association of Math Circles
http://www.mathcircles.org

National Consortium of Secondary STEM Schools (NCSSS)
http://www.ncsss.org

National Council of Supervisors of Mathematics
http://www.mathedleadership.org

National Council of Teachers of Mathematics
http://www.nctm.org

About the Authors

M. Katherine Gavin, Ph.D., is a gifted math education consultant, award-winning curriculum author, and retired associate professor at the Renzulli Center for Creativity, Gifted Education, and Talent Development at the University of Connecticut. She is the senior author and director of two national research projects, Projects M^3 and M^2, that involve the development of advanced mathematics units for mathematically talented students in grades K–5. These units have won the National Association for Gifted Children Curriculum Division Award for 9 consecutive years. Published by Kendall Hunt, they are used in all 50 states as well as internationally. A former mathematics teacher, department chair, and district coordinator, Dr. Gavin has written more than 100 articles, book chapters, and curriculum materials with a focus on gifted mathematics education, including coauthoring *Math Innovations*, a middle school mathematics program.

Joseph S. Renzulli, Ed.D., Distinguished Professor of Educational Psychology and Director of the Renzulli Center for Creativity, Gifted Education, and Talent Development, is an esteemed leader in gifted education whose contributions have had a profound impact on teachers and students. His work on the Three-Ring Conception of Giftedness, the Enrichment Triad Model, curriculum compacting, and the use of instructional technology to assess student strengths and match resources to students' electronic profiles were pioneering efforts to make the field more flexible and to place the focus on talent development. He has contributed hundreds of books, book chapters, articles, and monographs to the professional literature, many of which have been translated to other languages. The American Psychological Association named him among the 25 most influential psychologists in the world, and he recently received the Harold W. McGraw, Jr. Award for Innovation in Education, considered by many to be "the Nobel Prize" for educators.